Life after Bullying

Three Steps to Inner Peace

Lotte W. Vesterli

BALBOA
PRESS
A DIVISION OF HAY HOUSE

Balboa Press books may be ordered through booksellers or by contacting:

Balboa Press
A Division of Hay House
1663 Liberty Drive
Bloomington, IN 47403
www.balboapress.com
1 (877) 407-4847

Print information available on the last page.

ISBN: 978-1-9822-1695-5 (sc)
ISBN: 978-1-9822-1697-9 (hc)
ISBN: 978-1-9822-1696-2 (e)

Library of Congress Control Number: 2018914039

Balboa Press rev. date: 12/21/2018

Praise for Life After Bullying

"Bullying and its torturous consequences can affect us mentally, emotionally, physically, and spiritually. Lotte superbly guides us to move from victimhood to creator of our lives with clearly explained practices. Her wise guidance is a lifeline to anyone who has suffered from the unkind actions of others. Following her lead can result in deep relief, a life of peace, and a legacy of forgiveness toward those who did not know better or did not care."

Paul R. Scheele, Ph.D.
CEO of Scheele Learning Systems, co-founder
of Learning Strategies Corporation,
Developer of Paraliminals

"Are you someone who has been bullied? Do you know of someone who is being bullied? *Life After Bullying* is the perfect gift to yourself or to someone you care about. With such grace, Lotte Vesterli lovingly shares how she healed from the wounds of bullying to create the ideal life. With honesty, compassion, and skill, the author shows you practical exercises and tools that she has tested. You, too, can find your sacred self and create your ideal life after bullying. This book belongs in the hands of all of us who want to create a world where every child and adult is filled with confidence, sharing their gifts with their families and communities around the world."

Dr. Anita Sanchez
International trainer and speaker
Author of The Four Sacred Gifts: Indigenous
Wisdom for Modern Times.

"A brilliant book, chock-full of tools, tips and techniques for uplevelling your life! Lotte Vesterli has written a must-read masterpiece for anyone who's ever struggled with low self-esteem (and haven't we *all* at some point in life?)!"

Danne Reed
Author, Entrepreneur, Executive Producer –
Reignite Your Spark Tour,
Founder – Vellami.com

"The power of Lotte Vesterli's *Life After Bullying* comes from the power of her story and the immediate actions it provides to her readers. Most books of this type take half the pages explaining bullying, its history and why it is so bad for people based on statistics, research and global data. Lotte doesn't waste her time on this, as it doesn't take rocket science to know bullying is bad.

She immediately jumps into her incredible story and how she's transformed her life as a result of while sharing the gifts of her discoveries with her readers.

Life After Bullying is much more than Lotte's personal story, however. It is also a workbook that moves you through the steps of recovery and growth. Lotte has done a remarkable job of moving between storytelling and story doing where the exercises and activities help the reader create her own story.

Bullying is a topic that is on the tips of everyone's tongues these days. We see it in our schoolyards, experience it in the workplace and witness it in global politics. It is time for us to confront this unacceptable behavior on a personal basis so that we can cure it on a cultural basis. Lotte Vesterli's *Life After Bullying* is an important step towards that goal."

Richard S. Citrin, Ph.D., MBA
Author of The Resilience Advantage:
Stop Managing Stress and Find Your Resilience

"Lotte Vesterli is a wayshower. In *Life After Bullying,* she powerfully and courageously shares her journey from the victim of bullying to a woman in charge of her own life. Whether you've experienced one instance of bullying or decades, Lotte's experiences and the guidance she provides will help you reclaim your life."

Kathy Sparrow
Message Strategist, Author, and Founder of Writing at Your Edge

"I do not have enough words to praise this book highly enough. I was bullied without mercy when I was a child, and it left scars that lasted a lifetime. If this book had been available years ago, it would have changed my life completely.

Lotte endured terrible bullying and understands the pain and the damage it does to a child, and she shares her journey of how she began to overcome the abuse and to find her own power and voice.

Lotte beautifully and honestly shares her journey and reaches out her hand to help the rest of us follow her to a happier, healthier, more joyful life.

This is an amazing book, Lotte understands the pain suffered by people who have been bullied regardless of their age or place in life, and she offers simple but powerful suggestions about how to let go of the past, heal, and move on to a brighter future.

This book is healing, compassionate, encouraging and will change your life."

April Knight
Best-selling author and award-winning artist

To the love of my life, my husband Sten.
Without your support, this book would never have been written.

To Maria and Michael, my two wonderful children,
who continue to inspire me to keep growing.

Contents

Foreword xix

Preface xxi

Acknowledgments xxiii

Introduction xxv

    How to Use This Book xxvii

    Book Website xxvii

    I Would Love to Hear from You xxviii

Part One: Preparing the Ground 1

1 The Decision to Change 3

    The Day That Changed My Life 3

    The Best Decision I Have Ever Taken 4

    Be Ready to Change Your Life 5

    Unlocking the Door to Your Inner Self 6

    What Do You Want to Make Out of Your Life? 7

    Keep Track of Your Journey 8

    Summary 12

2 Take Ownership of Your Life 15

    Climbing to the Peak of Your Life 15

    Planning the Journey 18

    Taking Responsibility 22

    Choosing Your Life 24

    Believe in You 29

    Summary 34

3 Find Peace in You 37

Give the Power Back to Yourself 37

Freeing Up Your Energy 38

Be Open to Your Journey 39

What Is Holding You Back? 40

When You Feel You Don't Belong 45

What You Focus on Expands 46

Focus on the Mountaintop 48

You Are Capable of More Than You Think 50

Recognize Your Talents 51

Finding Peace in You 55

Play Games and Find Peace 55

Summary 59

4 Finding Your Voice 61

Get Comfortable with Your Voice 61

How Comfortable Are You with Your Voice? 62

Freeing Up Your Voice 62

Place Your Voice 64

Love Yourself and Raise Your Voice 66

The Journey to Love Yourself 68

Summary 72

Moving on to the Next Part of Your Journey 74

Part Two: Creating Your Blueprint for Success 75

5 Create the Future That's Fulfilling for You 77

Starting the Process 77

Creating Your New Life 78

Owning Your Goal 79

Adding Meaning to Your Life 83

Creating a Starting Point 88

Summary 89

6 **Creating Your Goal** **91**

The First Draft 91

The Power of Dreaming 92

Know What You Want 96

Setting Clear, Specific Goals 98

Summary 107

7 **Achieving Your Goal** **109**

Using Action Steps to Achieve Your Goal 109

Minimum/Target/Outrageous Goals 114

Envisioning Your Goal As Complete 116

Creating Reminders to Inspire Your Daily Actions 120

The Path to Achieve Your Goal 123

Summary 127

Part Three: Building Your Ideal Life 129

8 **Build Your New Life** **131**

Introduction to Part Three 131

In Honor of Your Progress 133

9 **Creating Time for You** **135**

When Pleasing Becomes Your Lifestyle 136

Get to Know How You Spend Your Time 137

Take Back Your Time 139

Make Your Life Important to You – Learn to Say "No" 141

Summary 143

10 Tap to Release 145

How Tapping Works. 146

The Procedure of Tapping. 148

The Power of Tapping 157

Summary 158

11 Regenerating Images in Memory (RIM) 159

How RIM Works. 160

Gaining New Insight Through Your Virtual Resource. 161

Summary 166

12 Breathe and Let Go 167

Moving into Relaxation 168

Relaxing and Letting Go 170

Harvest the Benefits of Meditation 173

Summary 176

13 Expand Your Comfort Zone. 177

Stepping Outside Your Walls 178

Feel Your Fear and Do It Anyway 180

Pushing Your Walls 181

Expanding Your Walls with the Tools in Your Toolbox. . . . 182

It's Not as Bad as You Think. 183

Action Plan 184

Summary 187

14 Physical Challenges and Personal Growth 189

Overcoming the Challenge 189

Getting the Right Support. 190

Benefits of Overcoming Physical Challenges 191

Taking up Your Challenge. 192

Summary 193

15 Learn from Your Life. **195**

Receiving Positive Feedback 195

Discarding Useless Feedback 196

Learning from Useful Feedback. 198

Accepting Feedback 199

Summary 200

16 Forgive to Move Forward **203**

Forgiving Others. 204

Forgiving Yourself 207

Summary 210

17 Transforming into The New You. **211**

Preparing Your New Self. 212

Taking Off 215

Dress for Success. 216

Creating Supportive Surroundings 217

Summary 218

18 Who Do You Surround Yourself With? **219**

Beware of the People Holding You Back. 220

The Five Most Important People in Your Life 220

How to Find Supportive People 222

Summary 223

19 Take the Next Step. **225**

Index **227**

About the Author. **235**

List of Exercises

Exercise 1: Commitment to the Process......................8

Exercise 2: Buy a Journal................................10

Exercise 3: Start Journaling 12

Exercise 4: Finding Yourself...............................20

Exercise 5: Changing Your Reactions.......................28

Exercise 6: Preparing for Success.........................33

Exercise 7: Uncover Your Limiting Beliefs..................41

Exercise 8: Acknowledge Your Current Situation.............44

Exercise 9: Notice How You Feel...........................49

Exercise 10: Discovering Your Uniqueness 52

Exercise 11: Placing Your Voice...........................64

Exercise 12: Mirror Exercise..............................69

Exercise 13: Find Meaning in Your Life 85

Exercise 14: Dream.......................................94

Exercise 15: Create a List of Your Deepest Wishes 96

Exercise 16: Setting a Clear and Measurable Goal 103

Exercise 17: Action Plan 113

Exercise 18: Minimum/Target/Outrageous Goals 115

Exercise 19: Envisioning Your Goal Achieved...............119

Exercise 20: Create Your Own Affirmation..................121

Exercise 21: How Do I Spend My Day?.....................137

Exercise 22: My Daily Life 140

Exercise 23: Enhance Your Voice..........................164

Exercise 24: Breathing to Relax 169

Exercise 25: Release Your Thoughts 172

Exercise 26: Relax and Let Go 174

Exercise 27: Take a Step Outside Your Comfort Zone 185

Exercise 28: Forgive and Let Go. 205

Exercise 29: Forgive Me for the Life I Have Created So Far. 208

Exercise 30: Transforming into The New You. 214

Exercise 31: Who Supports You? 221

Foreword

I have followed Lotte's amazing journey over the past seven years, and what she has achieved is incredible. When I first met her, Lotte suffered from serious social anxiety. Today she confidently leads workshops and speaks in front of large audiences. I have personally witnessed her living her dream as she powerfully supports others to heal from past traumatic experiences.

Lotte has written a remarkable book that might even change your life. She shares her personal journey and the effective tools she has discovered, developed and used. I happily recommend it to you.

As someone who knows what it feels like to be bullied, Lotte has suffered many of the typical consequences like learning problems, low self-worth, and eating disorder. At one painful point in her life, her voice became almost inaudible.

As an adult and young mother, she made a life-changing decision to put her fears aside and move forward. Seeking out tools and techniques that would help, she realized that letting go of her past meant healing from within. What she's personally learned is shared in *Life After Bullying* as a three-step method so others can heal much faster than she did. I am glad she is now sharing it in this book, so more people can benefit.

Lotte shares clear understandings and powerful exercises you can use to put your past behind you and start your own empowered journey. *Life After Bullying* also contains a strong toolbox of techniques you can use for the rest of your life, including an introduction to the RIM method, which I originated. RIM stands for "Regenerating Images in Memory," and I am thrilled that Lotte has trained to become an excellent RIM Master Practitioner and RIM Essentials Trainer.

This book will be helpful not only to people who have been bullied but to anyone who has suffered from traumatic experiences.

Follow Lotte's *Life After Bullying* process, do the exercises, use the tools and you can overcome any negative experiences from your past. Lotte knows that like her, you too can live the rich, fulfilling life you deserve. It's your turn!

Deborah Sandella, Ph.D., RN
#1 International Bestselling author of Goodbye Hurt & Pain, 7 Simple Steps to Health, Love and Success, [Conari Press]
Creator of RIM, a heavily-backed neuroscience tool proven to reduce stress and improve quality of life.
As seen in CNN, CBS, NBC, FOX and USA Today.

Preface

Tears streamed down my face. I saw before me a vivid vision of myself speaking to a crowd. I could see myself smiling with my head held high as I passionately shared my story. I could see people from all walks of life captivated as I spoke. I saw myself speaking at exotic places around the world, in big arenas and even a large open space in South Africa. The vision was so vivid and tangible it almost felt true.

Then anxiety rushed through my body. I was nearly paralyzed, and my palms became wet with sweat. The vision was so far outside my comfort zone. There was no way this could happen. Yet this was the vision I received in a guided meditation to show me my life purpose.

That same morning, I had to gather all the internal strength I could muster just to step into the large room with the other participants in the workshop. Every cell in my body screamed at me to run away. I finally managed to enter, and the next seven days would change my life forever.

I was dealing with low self-esteem and social anxiety. Speaking to strangers one-on-one was hard enough; speaking from a stage seemed impossible.

Since then, my life has changed dramatically. Today I know who I truly am. I confidently deliver workshops, speak on stage, and help individual clients all over the world. I live my passion, supporting people recovering from bullying and other traumatic events. The personal growth I have experienced has turned my life around.

One of the major shifts occurred when I realized even though I perceived myself as an extremely introverted, quiet person with nothing of interested to say, this wasn't the true me. Behind my shield, another Lotte was hidden. I still like quiet moments, but now also enjoy connecting and interacting with other people. I am more outgoing than I ever thought possible.

It has been several years since I was first inspired to write *Life After Bullying*. I wanted to show you that you are not born to be lonely or to hide in this world full of opportunities. No matter your age and how many years ago you were bullied, you have the power to turn your life around.

In *Life After Bullying*, I share my journey. It began slowly in 1996 and accelerated dramatically since that workshop in 2011. I have collected and documented the methods that have worked for my clients and me. Now I share them with you.

My goal with *Life After Bullying* is to give you a proven process with powerful exercises and many techniques you can use to turn your life around.

I hope you will take time to read *Life After Bullying* and give yourself permission to do the exercises. By doing so, you can heal. By healing yourself, you increase the quality of life for yourself and your family.

Welcome to the world of possibilities,

Lotte

Acknowledgments

Writing a book is a long process, and without the support of family and friends, I doubt that this book would ever have been written.

My husband for more than 20 years, Sten Vesterli, has been a fantastic support since the moment we met. He never doubted my ability to heal after being bullied and supported me throughout the whole journey. When the time came for me to write *Life After Bullying*, he encouraged me and helped me with great feedback and editing. Without him, this book would never have been completed.

My two children, Maria Vesterli and Michael Vesterli, have inspired me since their birth to keep improving to be a better mother. You have both been a driving force for me in my journey to heal from within.

I also want to thank Nete Bering Sahl for her drawings, my mastermind groups for inspiration and feedback, and my writing coach Christy Tryhus for getting me started.

Finally, I am grateful to my clients over the years. Your progress and growth has inspired me to write *Life After Bullying*.

Introduction

I invite you on a journey to a more powerful, fulfilling, and happy life. On the road, you will experience ups and downs. Sometimes, you might feel you are taking two steps forward and one step back. This journey also has the potential for you to experience more joy and fulfillment than you have ever imagined. When you persevere and keep moving forward, you will eventually get to the place you want to go.

My intention is to create a practical process to support you in overcoming your past and increasing your quality of life.

Life after Bullying is based on a three-step process that I have found to be the optimal way to support my clients, and I am happy to share it with you. It contains a natural progression and a toolbox you can use as you move forward in your healing process. There are three steps:

1. **Preparing the Ground**, where you create a strong foundation by acknowledging yourself and the knowledge you have acquired.

2. **Creating Your Blueprint for Success**, which guides you towards the right goal.

3. **Building Your Ideal Life**, where you learn tools to support you in creating your new life.

It is essential to work through Part One and Part Two and do the exercises, as it builds the foundation for your healing journey. When you have completed those, you move on to Part Three, which is designed as a toolbox. I have provided several tools for you. In my experience with many people, there is never one tool that fits all. My goal is that you will be able to pick one of the tools in Part Three that seem right for you now. When you have worked with your chosen tool for a while, revisit the toolbox and maybe try another one.

Part One: Preparing the Ground

Part One sets the starting point. To measure progress, you must know your starting point. If you started on a diet, you would weigh yourself to measure your progress. You do the same with your personal development by taking a deeper look at where you are today; both the parts you want to change and the things you do well today. I can assure you that there are things you do well already, even if you can't see them right away. To get started on the healing journey, it is important to create the foundation you will use to support you to keep moving forward.

Part Two: Creating Your Blueprint for Success

Part Two takes a look at the future. What is it you truly want to achieve? When you want to lose weight, you set a target that is your goal. When working on your personal goal, you will also set tangible sub-goals to measure the progress you are making. You are setting your internal GPS to prepare for your journey.

Part Three: Building Your Ideal Life

In Part Three you will find the tools to move through the roadblocks holding you back from reaching your destination. I have intentionally incorporated several tools you can pick and choose from throughout your journey. All these tools have worked for most of my clients, and I know they will help you too. Be aware that sometimes a tool does not resonate with you in the beginning. As you work with yourself, you might find that a tool you initially discarded becomes your new favorite. I recommend you first read through all the chapters and then try each tool for a minimum of one week before you move on to the next, and occasionally revisit the tool list as you grow.

How to Use This Book

This book is intended as a self-help book. You can use the book in two ways:

1. Start by reading through the entire book first and then start again from the beginning, doing each exercise
   or
2. Do the exercises as you go along while reading the book the first time.

Both ways are equally valid and effective. Some people prefer to establish a framework by reading the whole book first, and others prefer to dive straight into the journey.

As you move on, all I ask is that you be as open as you possibly can. With this attitude, you can't help but work from the inside out. You will be amazed at how much you are going to learn about yourself.

Book Website

Together with this book, I have created a companion website www.lifeafterbullying.com. Here you can find:

- A free workbook for download. This contains all the exercises, so you don't have to write in this book. The workbook also has more space and allows you to redo the exercises you want.

- Audio and video guides for some of the exercises and techniques in the book

- The online *Life After Bullying* course

- Links to additional resources

I Would Love to Hear from You

Feel free to write me with any questions you might have while reading this book and share your insights and progress. You can do this by sending me an email to lotte@lifeafterbullying.com.

I hope you will enjoy reading *Life After Bullying*, and especially hope that you will do the exercises so you can create a better life for yourself.

I honor you for being ready to take the next step; this openness is the beginning to a more fulfilling life.

Part One

Preparing the Ground

Chapter 1

The Decision to Change

"I was always looking outside myself for strength and confidence, but it comes from within. It is there all the time."

ANNA FREUD

The Day That Changed My Life

I will always remember that cloudy day as the day I decided to take charge of my own life. It was the 27th of January in 1996. I was tired of taking non-stop care of my seven-month-old son who was in the habit of waking up between six and eight times each night. More importantly, I was tired of not feeling good enough. I was tired of not being able to speak up, of never feeling that I could do anything right.

I made a firm decision to change the way I felt and acted. I wanted to be able to create the life I wanted, to be able to speak up and not feel anxiety every time I attended an event.

I was tired of being held back by my own limiting beliefs and fears. I wanted to change, but I didn't know how.

My story started many years before this day. Back in grade one, my primary teacher decided I was unable to learn. Why I don't know, but it impacted my life for many years to come.

The side effect of my teacher disliking me was that my classmates didn't want or dare to have anything to do with me either. Many times, I was left out. I was always chosen last for teams and not invited to their birthday parties. I felt alone, lost, and unwanted and incapable of anything. I started walking more and more slowly to school, dreading the hours I had to spend there. I hated every minute of it.

I didn't learn to read until I switched classes at the end of third grade. Unable to read, I had fallen behind in most other subjects as well. During the next years, I slowly caught up, finally leaving school with good marks. Intellectually, I had proof I was capable, but the harm was done and deeply embedded. In my heart, I didn't trust myself at all. I was sure I was no good; I had no self-esteem or self-worth and had no belief in my own talents.

I would mostly get high marks in written tests and very low scores in any oral exams. When I had to speak up, I would freeze, mumble, and hardly say a word. Today I talk about how I almost "lost my voice." Physically, I could speak. But I was so afraid of making a mistake I would mumble so quietly I was unintelligible.

I didn't like myself. It was hard for me to understand how other people could like me or even love me as my husband did.

The Best Decision I Have Ever Taken

I had spent the past 12 days taking care of our lovely seven-month-old baby, who unfortunately never slept much. My husband was working all week and attending training most weekends at his new job. I was so tired I could hardly function anymore. I was so desperate I decided to ask my husband to stay away from the training the following day to allow me to get some desperately needed sleep. A decision that – at that time – took a lot of courage, as I was usually afraid to speak up and claim what I needed.

But then something unexpected happened. My husband came home radiating with joy and excitement. He was so inspired and grateful for this training and couldn't stop talking about it. I love my husband. Of course, I didn't want him to miss out on training that made him so happy. As it turned out, my decision to keep my mouth shut was the best decision I ever made for myself.

Usually, we should stick to our decisions. Yet sometimes, our gut feeling tells us not to It is okay to be open and flexible, as long as the thing stopping you is not fear. We'll get back to how to handle fear in Part Three of this book.

The decision to trust my intuition ended up providing me with the answer I was looking for. I wanted to change but didn't know how. Where should I look? What were the tools and techniques I needed? Back in 1996, the Internet hardly existed for regular people. Denmark was not at the forefront of the nascent personal development trend, and new knowledge spread slowly and was difficult to find.

The next day my husband was told how he could continue his learning by buying a specific program from a company called Learning Strategies in the United States. As he received it, it came with a small booklet of other programs their company had developed, including one called "Anxiety Free." There was my answer. And because I had already made the choice to change, I was open to these new tools. It took several weeks for the audio cassettes to arrive by post (yes, it's that long ago). I started listening and began my journey to heal myself. Today, I believe that this long healing process is what made me the person I am today.

Be Ready to Change Your Life

Looking back over my journey, I can see why this specific day had such an impact on my life. I had made a firm decision to change and would not let my fear hold me back anymore. This decision primed me to look out for tools to help and support me, and I was ready to grab them as soon as I found them.

I know that you are ready too since you are reading this book. I am sure you have taken the same decision that I had made back then and are prepared to push through. Later in this chapter, you will find the first small yet significant step in your healing process.

To heal, you will need to unlock the emotions you are suppressing today. The more honest you are with yourself, the more you will realize you are already learning and growing. I know it can be hard to face some of these things that you suppress. But as you open even just a little, you are taking meaningful steps forward to regain your own power. There might be things that won't come forth at the beginning of your journey, and that is okay. They will reveal themselves when you are ready to work on them.

Unlocking the Door to Your Inner Self

Throughout my journey, I have unlocked several layers within myself. For each layer revealed, I have gained a more profound sense of freedom and love for myself and others. For each layer, I have felt a sense of sincere appreciation of how far I have come. Looking back, I can see how many steps I have taken. I know my whole life is a journey and I will keep expanding and growing.

I am not saying it was easy. Sometimes I felt I hadn't accomplished anything for a long time. Then, over a few weeks, I would have an insight where I experienced the change. Realize these moments are essential as they support you in your process.

During my journey, I did not have a guide. I collected tools as I went along, starting with Paraliminal cassette tapes from Learning Strategies, and moving on to more expansive home study programs, seminars, in-person workshops, and one-on-one sessions. I have included a list of some of the resources I used on the book website.

With *Life After Bullying*, I have put together a comprehensive, step-by-step process designed after my own healing journey and the journeys of my clients. My intention is to help you move forward and improve your life as quickly and efficiently as possible. This book contains powerful and effective tools I have found and created to help you realize your full potential.

What Do You Want to Make Out of Your Life?

Your life is what you make of it. This means every step you take to move forward takes some work and commitment from you. At the same time, it is some of the most rewarding and beneficial work for your inner growth. Being willing to push through and move forward no matter what will change your life. As you stick with the book and take one step at a time, it will become easier. This journey is not about speed, but about consistency.

Remember that a baby must learn to crawl before it can walk and walk before it can run. The same is true when you go through a major transformation where you heal from the past and let the true you come forward.

When Michelangelo carved the beautiful David statue, people were amazed and asked how he had done it.

Michelangelo answered that he "carved away everything that did not look like David."

Your negative beliefs, anxiety, and internal pain are not you. For you to become whole, you must carve away everything that does not look like you, feel like you, or in any other way is not what you want to be.

7

This is a slow process of improvement, like Michelangelo chipping away at a massive block of marble. Remember, for every piece you carve away, more of the true you will shine through.

Remember you are a powerful human being. Both you and your family deserve you to start your healing process and inner growth.

Exercise 1: Commitment to the Process

Commit to working through this book and doing the exercises. When you make a firm commitment, you are more likely to follow through, and less likely to put the book aside when you feel it gets a little difficult. If you are ready to commit to doing the exercises, allow your commitment to be embedded on a deeper level by signing up below.

I hereby commit to working through the exercises in *Life after Bullying* to honor myself and create the life I deserve.

Date: _____

Signature: _____

Now that you have made a commitment it is time to start being aware of your progress.

Keep Track of Your Journey

I was sitting with a client. A couple of weeks before I had guided her through an exercise where she had achieved some critical insight. Now, she felt devastated. She didn't feel any change.

I asked her about her sleep, which had been one of her primary issues. She told me she had been sleeping much better. She had fewer flashbacks and was not waking up as many times as she used to. When she realized this was a serious improvement, she understood the work she was doing was really supporting her personal growth.

It can be difficult to see the improvement when it comes gradually. Your sleep might slowly be improving, or you might be feeling more at ease among other people.

We notice our discomfort. When life flows more easily, we often forget to take notice. Therefore, it is vital to keep track of your journey, so that you can become aware of your improvement and keep going.

How to Note Your Improvement

The best way to keep track is in a personal journal. The journal is for your eyes only. Your journal is a place where you can list all your achievements – big and small – that matter to you. Besides keeping track of your improvement, it's a place where you can feel free to dream big dreams, to jot down the things you want to change, and to set goals.

Your journal is not for evaluating, but merely a place to list everything you can think of. Nothing is too trivial or simple. Every little goal and win has a place in the larger order of things.

Furthermore, journaling opens your eyes to the positive things in your life you can be grateful for. In the beginning, you might feel there is nothing positive at all. As you open your awareness, you will discover you have more to be grateful for than you realize.

You have food on your table, while not everyone in this world can get enough to eat. You have electricity, maybe a car, a home, kids? Or you might just happen to pass by some colorful flowers on the way to work. Start noticing the small things and the rest will come.

Buy a nice-looking journal that you can feel attached to. It does not have to be expensive – all that matters is that you like it and can feel inspired to write in it every day.

Another important part of journaling is that it supports you to stay on the journey. When you keep track of your improvements, you can look back on your wins on days where you don't feel anything is happening. Often you will reach an awareness that you have indeed changed, and your work to heal yourself is helping you on a deep level.

Exercise 2: Buy a Journal

Buy a nice-looking personal journal. It is, of course, possible to keep a journal on your computer, but I recommend against that. Please use a paper journal to keep track of your progress, to list your goals, and write answers to the exercises in this book. Handwriting creates a link in our brain that typing on a keyboard doesn't do. This causes us to be more aware of our progress on an unconscious level.

Commit to buying your journal at the first opportunity and set a date to have purchased your journal here.

By _____ / _____ / 20_____ I will have bought my journal and have started my transformation.

Now that you have your journal, I recommend you divide it up like this:

- The first 10 pages to list your goals and affirmations.
- The last 10 pages to keep track of the milestones (see below).
- The middle part is your everyday diary, where you list small wins and things you are grateful for.

Milestones are the markers that prove to you beyond any doubt that you have made major progress. There are two types of milestones: Planned and spontaneous.

Planned milestones are goals you plan and then achieve.

Spontaneous milestones are episodes where something makes you realize you have changed significantly toward a more powerful you. As an inspiration, I will share some of my milestones as we go through this book.

Exercise 3: Start Journaling

Now that you have your journal, it is time to get started. Remember to set aside the first 10 pages to list your goals and affirmations and the last 10 pages to record your milestones.

Get into the habit of using your journal daily. Write down the positive things you have noticed during the day. This can be everything from noticing how green the grass is to something like, *"Even though my boss yelled at me I could see how it was all about him and not me, and I was able to stay centered and work through the pain it had created using some of my new tools."*

Write briefly, but with enough detail to be able to recognize the episode when you read your journal later.

In the diary part, you can also note every inspiration you get along the way and anything you want to remember. Your journal is a great book to keep handy as you read this book and work through the exercises.

Summary

Congratulations on making the commitment to take responsibility for your own happiness and to start on the journey to healing yourself.

Remember to keep track of your progress as you go along. Write in your journal daily and celebrate every little win. If you experience a setback, take a deep breath, exhale, and decide to keep going.

Remember that *Part One* is about preparing the ground by creating a strong foundation. *Part Two* is about designing the future you want to create a blueprint for success. *Part Three* is a toolbox that will provide you with a variety of tools to support your success.

In the next chapter, you will make sure you know your starting point and start the process of building a strong foundation. This is when you begin to change from the inside out and create your new you.

I hope you have already bought a journal to write down your exercises and insights. If not, at least have a piece of paper and a pencil at hand as you continue reading. Capturing your thoughts as you go along is an integral part of the healing process.

Lotte's Strategies to Increase Your Quality of Life

> ✔ Commit to the change you want.
>
> ✔ Write in your journal every day; 3 things or more that you are grateful for.
>
> ✔ Keep track of your success and internal wins in your journal.

Chapter 2

Take Ownership of Your Life

"Peak performance begins with your taking complete responsibility for your life and everything that happens to you."

BRIAN TRACY

Climbing to the Peak of Your Life

I gasped in the thin air as I struggled up the narrow track towards the Thorung La pass. We were in the Annapurna region of Nepal at almost 18,000 feet altitude, high in the Himalaya Mountains. My boyfriend and I were struggling up the twisting path, not knowing what was waiting around the next corner.

My own recovery journey looks a lot like that trip. It was often a struggle to take the next step in the steep mountains of the Himalaya. But whenever you reached the next plateau, the view was breathtaking and well worth the effort. The same is true for my recovery: I've had a journey with ups and downs. Often, it wasn't easy. But whenever I reached a new level, I was fully able to enjoy the new life I had achieved.

Your Climbing Partner

The Annapurna Circuit is a grueling trek that takes a minimum of 21 days. Not everybody makes it around the towering Annapurna massif. Having to pause for breath literally every four steps, I also contemplated turning around. What stopped me was the thought of the twelve-day hike back down the Manang valley, knowing I had been defeated. And the fact that I was traveling with my boyfriend, a friend who was able to see my true self and love me as I was. I didn't want to let him down.

My husband has always been a big support. I have cried on his shoulder when I felt I was not moving forward at all. And we have laughed and celebrated every small win throughout my journey.

It was especially critical for me to have his support when visiting family and old friends. People who have known you for a long time will view you as you were before you started your transformation. You risk falling into your former role and behavior. My husband's support helped me see what was happening, so I could hold on to the new behaviors I had learned. For many years, he was my only support. Without him, I probably wouldn't have reached where I am today.

I encourage you to find someone to support you on your climb. It can be a close friend you trust, your partner, a grown-up child or even a coach. Today I have the support of mentors, friends, and online communities where we talk about our experiences, share our wins, and support each other during difficult times.

Keep Moving Forward

When you are on a hard journey, it can be tempting to stop and turn back, to accept defeat. Remember life is created moment by moment. Whenever you push through and keep going, you win. Even a small step in the right direction is a huge win. The primary thing is to move forward at the right pace for you in any given moment.

Whenever you are tempted to give up, look back at what you have accomplished already, even if you do not feel it is very much. If you keep a journal, you can look through old entries. Own the fact your life is moving forward. Know when you keep taking action to change your life, you will keep growing.

We started our trek just before sunrise and reached the pass just before noon. The view was breathtaking, but I was utterly spent. As we sat down to rest, I fell asleep against a rock. I needed the break. After a short nap, we started our descent towards Muktinath far below.

Around us was only ice, snow, and rocks. We had to get down to a lower and warmer altitude before we could fill our water bottles again. As darkness fell, we were still struggling through the inhospitable zone above 5,000 meters.

With sharp drops on both sides of the rocky spur we were following, it was too dangerous to continue. We made camp as best we could, lying close together under a tarp and munching our last pieces of chocolate.

After a cold and thirsty night under the brilliant stars, sunrise finally allowed us to continue.

Sometimes, it is better to take a break than to keep struggling along. Your break can be as short as 5 minutes to stop and think about which action to take next. Granting yourself this breathing space is often enough to allow you to continue forward.

As I walked in the Himalayas, we often followed narrow paths with a drop of several hundred feet to one side. I had to look down, taking slow, deliberate steps and concentrating on the track immediately ahead. My internal fear would often almost block me. But whenever I took a break of a few minutes and looked around, the sight of the mountains around me made the struggle worthwhile.

My journey towards my own recovery was similar. There were many times I felt fearful and unable to move on. But taking short breaks always gave me the strength to take the next step.

17

You might feel that you are walking in a dark valley right now, feeling low and unworthy. And yet you know there is an alternative to the life you live today. Because you are reading these words, I know you are ready to start the climb towards the light and powerful you. And I know you can do it.

It is normal to sometimes feel like giving up. Your internal fear will pop its head up occasionally. Keep pushing, and you will eventually get the results you desire. This journey is not about moving quickly. On the contrary, it is about creating lasting results. That usually means taking small steps and keeping on walking at your own speed. In this chapter, you get a few exercises to start this journey. In Part Three I expand on these and give you several other tools to support you in pushing through internal fear.

Planning the Journey

When we decided to walk the steep steps of Himalaya, we prepared for the journey. We knew we would be on our own at high altitude and there was a risk of something going wrong. The better prepared you are, the easier it will be to push through when obstacles get in the way.

Creating a Strong Foundation

Preparing for success involves building a strong foundation. To establish this, you need to truly know where you are today. This includes both your strengths and your weaknesses. This step can feel painful. Skipping it is tempting. Please don't.

It is crucial because it gives you the insight you need to establish a plan for creating lasting results. Once you have taken stock of where you are today, you have a great reference you can look back on later to see how far you have come.

Going through the "Finding Yourself" exercise below prepares you to take ownership of your life. Do you want to stay where you are today? Or do you want to change?

Owning your own life means knowing who you really are today. This gives you a strong starting place as you commit to changing your life for good.

Start by writing down deeply and openly where you see yourself and your situation today. Write as much as you can right now. Later in this part of the journey, I will invite you to expand on this and acknowledge the things you are doing a good job on today. These things might be hard to see when your self-worth is low.

How Do You See Yourself?

When I started my journey, I saw myself as a person not worthy of life. I was afraid to interact with other people. At parties, I would hide in the kitchen being the nice girl offering to help. I was escaping to the kitchen to avoid the crowd.

I saw myself as someone nobody wanted to be around, and as someone nobody wanted to hear from. I thought I couldn't achieve any goals.

I believed that I couldn't change my situation. I was stuck being who I had become, with low self-esteem and self-worth. I thought there was nothing to do and I just had to live with this feeling.

Until my healing process started with a self-help cassette tape, I thought the person I was at that time was the genuine me. I did not realize I was formed by my experience. The real and powerful me was hiding deep inside my body, not able to push through the image I had created of myself.

Luckily, my negative self-image has proved not to be true. As you work through this book, you will discover much of what you think about yourself is also not true.

How do you see yourself today? Write it down in the following exercise.

This is your starting point. From here, you will move forward as you work through the exercises.

Exercise 4: Finding Yourself

Set aside at least half an hour of quiet time to do this exercise. Turn off your phone and other notifications. If you like, play relaxing music in the background.

Answer the following questions as deeply and openly as you can. Please write your answers before continuing. If you are unable to write right now, make a commitment to do it as soon as possible by scheduling time for it in your calendar.

Remember you don't have to share your writing with anyone. These questions and your answers serve to make you more aware of where you are today, so you can move forward effectively. Your answers also establish a baseline to make it easier for you to recognize your inner changes as you move forward.

How do you see yourself today?

(Examples: Are you quiet or outgoing? Nervous, anxious, self-centered? What is your current level of self-worth? Do you feel comfortable with your body?)

_____

_____

_____

_____

_____

How do you see your situation today?

(Examples: Do you hide at home, only leaving the house when you have to? How is your relationship with your family? Friends? Co-workers? How do you sleep at night? Do you share your knowledge, or do you tend to stay quiet?)

_____

_____

_____

_____

_____

Taking Responsibility

Now you have identified your current situation, the next step is to commit to making changes in your beliefs, actions, and life. These changes can only come from you. You need to accept the responsibility for changing your life.

Stop Allocating Blame

Going through the internal struggle in my life, it was easy for me to put all the blame on my first teacher. Since those first grades, I had lacked trust in others and, even worse, in myself. I had a hard time believing in myself, struggled with anxiety, and struggled to get friends. I blamed my teacher because in my eyes she was the demon who had ruined my life.

Allocating blame like that made me feel there was a good reason for my feelings and the struggle I went through. I didn't even consider that things could be different. The fact was I didn't really want to face reality. I was letting my inner belief, and internal fear hold me down instead of taking responsibility for my life and change.

It took me almost 25 years to truly realize I had a choice. On an intellectual level, you might know change is necessary and that you are capable of it. But until you feel it in your heart, it is tough to start the transformation. Because you are reading this, I know you have reached the point where you feel the need to change. Congratulations on making this decision.

There is no need to feel that mental pain anymore, to feel blocked, unable to move forward. Know that life can be full of joy and compassion if you make the shift.

You might think you should have made this change long ago. The timing is not relevant. It took me many years to get to the place I am today. When I started, the long-term effect of bullying was not well known. It was hard to find self-development help, and the Internet was in its infancy.

You need to know what you don't know to find solutions. Today, even though everything seems to be available on the Internet, we still need to know what we are looking for to find answers.

Today Is the Time to Start

I have been growing and learning since my early thirties, and yet my major breakthrough didn't come until I was in my forties. That's when all the pieces finally came together, and I am now able to live my own life fully and do what I dream of: supporting other people heal much faster and easier than I did.

It is never too late. I know people who started doing this work in their sixties and seventies and are now living a life of much higher quality than before. We don't know how many years we have left, so we should choose to live all of them to our full potential.

One of my grandmothers lived past 100. She was deeply involved with the SOS Children's Villages and promoted their work through public speaking until she was 93 years old. She was vision impaired and didn't walk well, but that didn't stop her doing what she was passionate about.

When I worked as an occupational therapist, I helped a young man diagnosed with brain cancer. He was just 30 years old when he died.

You might have 10, 20, 50 or even more years left. Choose to make the best of every day, week, month, and year.

Choosing Your Life

It is time to make a choice and take full responsibility for your life no matter what you have gone through. You owe it to yourself to live the rest of your life to your highest potential. And to own your life as it is today is a key to moving forward. Let me explain.

Becoming Aware

Whatever you experience leads to an outcome. Being bullied or in other ways traumatized might cause the outcomes of anxiety, stress, feeling unworthy, or not capable. The result is determined by your reaction to the experience. Changing your response to the event makes a big difference in how you integrate the experience into your being.

I am often asked how you can change your reaction to being bullied. Knowing that you have a choice in any situation helps. As you grow internally, you will start asking yourself different questions about situations.

My teacher chose me as a target without even knowing if I was capable of learning. Did she do it because I was stupid? Probably not. Maybe the way I looked triggered something in her from one of her own earlier experiences. I don't know. But the whole situation was in all likelihood more about her than about me.

Looking back from where I am today, I can see that. This does not excuse what my teacher did, but it gives me the power to move through what happened and raise my self-esteem. When I stopped blaming my teacher and changed the way I looked at the situation, my healing started.

You must stop blaming others and, most importantly, stop blaming yourself. Blaming and complaining about a situation doesn't change it, but it does prevent you from moving forward. I know this is easy to say and hard to do. Just make a conscious decision to *be aware of whether you are blaming someone or yourself, and then choose to think differently.*

To train your mind to help you when you become aware you are blaming is to say in your mind: "Stop. I choose to learn from this. The way I will react differently next time is…"

Taking responsibility for your own life and being able to really let go of your past requires you to stop blaming yourself and others. In Part Three, you will learn how you can forgive both yourself and others to make it easier to stop the blaming. Raising your conscious awareness of your reaction and deciding to be open to change it is the first step.

You Have a Choice

Jack Canfield, who is a very successful coach and one of my mentors, explains this with a simple formula:

Event + Reaction = Outcome

When you change your reaction to the event, you create a different outcome.

Coming home after another day in school where I felt I didn't belong, I went to the kitchen, grabbed a plate, and filled it with food. Back in my room, I opened a book and escaped into its world, munching away as I tried to forget my misery. Afterward, I threw up in order not to gain any more weight than I already had. I blamed myself for being unable to control myself but would find myself doing the exact same thing after the next bad day at school.

Like many other bullying victims, I struggled with my weight. I went on various diets. At the same time, I would comfort eat whenever I felt bad about myself and my limiting beliefs. I blamed myself for my lack of self-control, not realizing that the blaming made it all worse. The event was "comfort eating," the reaction was "blaming myself," and the outcome was "losing even more of my already low self-esteem." I was unable to break out of this downward spiral until I stopped blaming myself.

When I forgave myself for my habit of comfort eating, I found I was suddenly able to make more healthy choices without really thinking about it. I saw myself grabbing less junk food and more crackers, carrots, and other healthier things. I would cut it up into small bites, so it took more time to munch it. Slowly I was able to change my habit. Now the formula was working to my benefit. The event was still "comfort eating," but now the reaction was "accepting and forgiving myself," and the outcome was healthier choices. This stopped the downward spiral, and I was slowly able to change my habit, raising my self-esteem, and finally overcoming my addiction to comfort eating.

Comfort eating is a common habit for people with low self-esteem and can lead to bulimia and anorexia. It feels good in the moment but immediately leads to self-blame. Nevertheless, sufferers do it over and over.

Being overweight is a way of shielding your true self from the world behind a physical barrier of extra body fat. This is true for people who have been harmed in different ways and is especially common among people who have been bullied or sexually abused. As you raise your self-esteem, it will become easier for you to lose weight next time you set a weight-loss goal.

Making Better Decisions

Moving through life making clear choices on how to react will change the outcome of any situation. This is an ongoing process, and no-one does it perfectly. Our reactions are often spontaneous but becoming conscious of them is the key.

It doesn't matter how you react, as long as you can use it as a learning experience. Reflect on the situation and notice how you reacted. Extract the learning from this reaction and visualize a different response next time a similar event occurs.

Instead of blaming yourself for over-eating, becoming angry or some other negative behavior, think of what you could have done differently. Make a mental decision how you will react differently the next time. Appreciate yourself for creating awareness about your reactions. You have spent all your life until now training your current responses. It is natural it will take a while to change them. Don't quit because you fail one time. Start again, keep going and as you grow internally, you will notice that you start to react differently.

Are you ready to take ownership of your life and look more deeply at your reactions to the events of your life?

Exercise 5: Changing Your Reactions

Think back over the past weeks: Where have you not taken full responsibility for your life? Come up with a least one event where you could have reacted differently to create another outcome. It is most useful if you can think of an event that is likely to happen again.

Write down what happened and how you reacted:

_____

_____

_____

_____

_____

Think of how you can change your reaction to create another outcome. Write this new reaction down:

_____

_____

_____

_____

_____

Now make the internal shift by closing your eyes, thinking back at the situation and imagining reacting the new way you just came up with. Feel the experience in your body and sense your reaction to the new outcome. Visualize and feel the experience as best as you can. When you are really feeling how you can react this new way, enhance the feeling by pressing your ring finger and thumb together. To increase this, even more, you can choose to do this visualization every day for a least one week.

Note that our body can't tell the difference between a lived experience and a visualized experience. Sometimes, this can hold us back when we accidentally picture an imaginary negative outcome of an upcoming event.

But this is also a great power we can use to envision how we react differently and successfully to an upcoming event. Doing this kind of visualization will support us the next time we are in the real situation because we have already experienced it in our minds.

Believe in You

Beliefs automatically reinforce themselves. If your beliefs are limiting, this mechanism works against you. But as you replace your limiting beliefs with positive, life-enhancing beliefs, these will also reinforce themselves, putting you on a powerful upward trajectory.

Accept Your Fears

I was standing on a mountain slope high above Chamonix in the French Alps. My heart raced as I waited for my turn. The paraglider before me effortlessly lifted off into the crisp mountain air, and now it was my turn.

Taking a deep breath, I took a step forward. I heard the rustle of nylon as my paraglider filled with air. I glanced up and saw the brightly colored canopy above me. For a brief moment, I could either pull down on the brake lines and stop, or I could trust the thin fabric to carry me. I pushed forward and soared into the air.

Believing that you can't do anything right and cannot achieve your dreams is like creating one big obstacle that stands in the way of achieving any success in your life. How many times have you held yourself back from doing something you wanted to do because you believed you were doomed to failure? How many times have you not applied for a job or training because you did not believe you would get it? How many times have you chosen safety instead of taking a chance and trying something different? Not believing in yourself is the number one thing that holds people back from achieving their dream and goals.

Getting Your Brain to Help

It is important that you trust yourself and believe you can achieve the things you set yourself up to. Believing you can do something sets you up for success. Believing you can't sets you up for failure. Having a supportive buddy helps, but you can do it on your own if you marshal your internal power.

Science shows that when you believe and can see yourself accomplishing your goal, your chances of success increase dramatically.

Belief is not magic; if you have never run before and you start out on a marathon without any prior training, your chances of success are less than 1%. On the other hand, even well-trained runners who harbor doubts are much more inclined to quit when the going gets tough around the 20-mile mark. First-time marathon runners who have both trained and visualized succeeding have a probability of running past the finish line of more than 95%.

You can still be stopped by outside factors like a sprained ankle. If that happens, you heal and make a new attempt. Being stopped by some physical issue does not affect your feeling of self-worth the same as quitting due to a mental block.

It is easy to make the decision to believe in yourself. The hard part is keeping this belief alive day to day. This is an ongoing process, and you need to train your "belief" muscle to achieve greater success, self-esteem, and self-worth. Just like your legs get stronger when you run more, you strengthen your belief in yourself by constant practice.

Training Your "Belief" Muscle

Most of the exercises throughout this book are designed to support you in strengthening your "belief" muscle. The idea is to help you keep expanding your positive belief about yourself and to shred your limiting beliefs.

To support the process, make sure you keep your journal where you can write down every time you push yourself through a limiting belief. Note your successes and any new insights you gain in the process.

Here is a simple exercise to start strengthening your "belief" muscle. You can use this to support you in your daily life to create a turnaround for an upcoming situation. This exercise can be used before you attend a meeting, go to a party, give a presentation, or have dinner with your in-laws.

The exercise shifts your mindset about an upcoming situation. For some people it works wonders the first time they do it; for others, it takes a little practice. Remember to notice even the slightest change in your mindset and body posture as you complete the exercise. You can do the exercise several times in a row. Don't push yourself but be open to any experience you have. Know that life is a journey and little by little you strengthen your "belief" muscle.

To perform the exercise, imagine an upcoming situation you feel uncomfortable about. For example, you might be going to a party where you are afraid you will feel insecure and where you don't believe you can have fun. Now take a deep breath and become aware of your body. As you center your attention, think about the situation again and use a statement starting with, "I choose to believe…"

For the party example, say, "I choose to believe I can have fun."

Notice the difference in your body. Using the words, "I choose to," or even, "Just for now I choose to," gives the body the feeling of possibility.

For this exercise, I have chosen the words, "I choose to," instead of, "I can." This is based on my experience with many clients, some of whom get stuck trying to think, "I can." If the sentence you say feels too far away from your current belief, your body resists the training. You bypass this potential block by using the less aggressive, "I choose to believe," simply leaving open the possibility of experiencing the change.

This exercise expands on the earlier exercise where you worked on the reactions you have already had to create a better response to the situation next time. In this exercise, you are focusing on an *upcoming* event you feel uncomfortable about.

Exercise 6: Preparing for Success

1. Make yourself comfortable in a place where you can be undisturbed for a few minutes and can safely close your eyes. Before you start, read through the whole exercise.

2. Select an upcoming event that is likely to contain a task you believe you can't do.

3. Be clear what it means for you to be able to do it, and what it will look like to accomplish this specific thing.

4. Choose to believe you can by stating, "Just for now. I choose to believe I can accomplish (whatever it is you want.)" Be specific about the accomplishment.

5. Close your eyes and visualize yourself accomplishing this situation and feeling good as you do so. Add as many details as you can: What do you hear? See? Taste? Smell? Feel? Observe? Do you see a supporting look on other people's faces? Maybe you sense how you receive a high five? Perhaps the applause from the crowd in front of you? Maybe being part of an engaging conversation around the dinner table? Whatever it is, make sure it feels right and empowering.

Give yourself a few minutes to really experience the upcoming event in your mind's eye.

1. Now take a few deep cleansing breaths and let the vision be part of you. Fully own it and know you can do it.

2. Anchor the vision when the change feels real and empowering. Do this by pressing your thumb and ring finger together. This serves as an anchor, and whenever you do this physical movement during the event, your body will remember the vision connected to you and the event.

3. You can go back to the vision any time during the event when you feel you need the support of the vision.

Note that this process can take a little practice in the beginning. You might want to set aside 10 minutes to go through this exercise at first. As you get used to the procedure, you can do it in as little as 3-4 minutes and will benefit from doing it even if you have only one minute.

Remember our minds can't tell the difference between a visualized event and a real event; this is why we can use this exercise to strengthen ourselves.

Do this exercise daily, thinking of the next upcoming event you feel anxious about, and you will soon experience the benefit.

Summary

As you embark on this journey, you are ready to take ownership of your life. You know everything that has happened to you over the years has shaped you and led you to the life you live today.

You now know you have more resources and skills than you might have thought, and who you are today is just fine. Now it is time to take the next step and open up to a more fulfilling and powerful life. This means starting your internal growth and changing your limiting beliefs about yourself and what you are capable of. With the exercises in this chapter, you have already begun.

In the next chapter, we will look more into how you can create inner peace to support your internal growth.

Lotte's Tip: Good, Better, Best

I have studied the ancient Chinese health practice called Qigong for many years and have had the privilege to study with master Chunyi Lin. Whenever a student was feeling anxious if he or she was doing the movements right, Master Lin always said: "There are no mistakes, only good, better, and best."

I have taken this advice to heart in everything I do and teach. Knowing that at least I learn what to do differently next time has often made the difference for me and given me the push to take a leap and move forward.

I encourage you to think the same way. Pushing through is always good, no matter the outcome. You are learning and growing. Not everything is easy, and you will make mistakes as I have done and still do. Acting and learning is always at least good, often better, and sometimes best.

Keep this statement in mind as you go through your life:

"There are no mistakes, only good, better, and best."

Lotte's Strategies to Increase Your Quality of Life

- ✔ Have someone you trust, who can support you on your journey.

- ✔ Take full responsibility for your life.

- ✔ Believe you can do it.

- ✔ Train your "belief" muscle and prepare for success.

- ✔ Keep moving. Even small steps make a big difference in the long run.

- ✔ Remember the saying, "There are no mistakes only good, better, and best.

Chapter 3

Find Peace in You

"To be beautiful means to be yourself. You don't need to be accepted by others. You need to accept yourself."

THICH NHAT HANH

Give the Power Back to Yourself

How often have you been told that you should, "just accept your past and move forward"? I've heard this statement many times, and I just didn't get it.

How could I possibly accept that I had been bullied by my teacher and my classmates?

How could I accept that I was a quiet, timid girl who had almost lost her voice, who often felt insecure and didn't trust herself at all?

I truly believed that those people who told me to accept my current situation had to be crazy. Today I know that accepting my current situation is not about liking my situation or agreeing that it was okay for people to bully me.

What accepting my current situation truly means is simply this: That I am willing to acknowledge this is where I am in my life – in this very moment. That it is okay to be me. I have done the best I could up until now with the knowledge and skills that I had. And **now** I am ready to move forward.

When I truly got this vital lesson, I was able to move on in my life.

*It is okay to be me right here in this moment
and I acknowledge all my feelings about myself right here, right now.*

There are two critical points here:

1. I was ready to accept the situation I was in right in that moment.
   and
2. I wanted to move forward and create the life I desired.

What I am telling you is *not,* "Just accept your past." I am telling you to acknowledge yourself as you are today with everything that has happened to you.

When you acknowledge yourself and your current situation, you give power to yourself and take it away from your former bullies. And this alone is a huge step moving forward. You are putting yourself in charge and showing your inner self that, "Yes, I am ready to change my life."

Freeing Up Your Energy

One great thing that comes from choosing to acknowledge yourself as you are in any given moment is that it frees up energy. Before acknowledging yourself, you spend a lot of energy on hiding your inner beliefs. You pretend you are someone else and don't let your true emotions shine through.

Most of this hiding from your own feelings happens unconsciously. Most of us suppress our emotions, especially if we are low on self-esteem and self-worth. To grow, we must learn to become aware of this.

It is tough to work on and release feelings we won't accept we have. It is like our body won't open up to release these feelings. This is part of why it is so important to acknowledge your feelings whenever you notice them.

I will remind you of this when I go through the different ways you can help yourself. When you acknowledge yourself, you can get down to the core of the issue, to the foundation where true healing lies.

Be Open to Your Journey

There is one thing I want you to be aware of: it is very hard to acknowledge or accept your situation right here and now, and then never look back. Few people can do this. For the rest of us, it is an ongoing process, and you are just starting. It didn't happen overnight for me, and it probably won't happen overnight for you either. This is totally fine. Each time you take one step and acknowledge your situation in any given moment, you have moved one step forward.

Know that who you are is a combination of how you were born and what you have gone through. Each time you feel it is okay to be you and that everything is going to be all right, you are moving forward.

Don't beat yourself up. We are always doing the best we can with the awareness and knowledge that we have. You might find some of the steps you will learn here seem so easy you should have discovered them yourself earlier. Just acknowledge you are now ready to change and that is wonderful.

As you step more and more into this acceptance of yourself, you might even notice you start to share your story, and you own how your story has given you depth and wisdom. Right now, the most crucial question is: *Are you willing to take the step to accept your life today as it is?* I can promise you that as you practice, it will become easier.

What Is Holding You Back?

Before you move into doing the next exercise, let's discuss limiting beliefs. A limiting belief is one you have about yourself, and which doesn't serve you. Limiting beliefs hold you back from living fully and achieving your goals. Usually, we are not consciously aware of our limiting beliefs and don't truly know what is blocking us from moving forward.

When you have limiting beliefs, you think they are correct, and they are embedded deep in your body on the cellular level. Just as I believed I was stupid even though I could see my grades were above average. Luckily, there are many options today to turn these limiting beliefs around.

The limiting beliefs we hold towards ourselves can reach a point where we don't feel worthy of living. If you feel this way – STOP. Know that you can turn your life around. You are worthy of living. The struggle you are going through right now will make you a better person with more wisdom and knowledge. And with the ability to support others moving forward.

I have been in a place where I thought about suicide. That is not a nice place to be. Luckily, I was able to stop myself by thinking of the grief my family would endure. Today, I have a life that is worth living. Today I live my passion: To help you to move through your current situation and live a life worth living.

> *If you are at a point where suicide feels like the best option –*
> *Seek help at once.*
>
> *Search for "Suicide hotline" on Google or another search*
> *engine.*
>
> *The Wikipedia article "List of suicide crisis lines" contains*
> *numbers to call in many countries.*

Learning your limiting beliefs supports your personal growth. As you become aware of them, you can turn your limiting beliefs around. In Chapter Two you started to uncover your beliefs about yourself. The following exercise will support you in digging deeper into discovering your limiting beliefs. It also trains your mind and opens your awareness to what's holding you back in various situations. Do yourself a favor and come back to this exercise regularly.

Each time you go through this exercise, you dig a little deeper, move forward and open up to your true self.

Exercise 7: Uncover Your Limiting Beliefs

Read through the whole exercise before you start. Set aside half an hour to make sure you have plenty of time available. Turn off your phone and make yourself comfortable. Do not do this exercise while driving or operating machinery.

This exercise opens your awareness to new thoughts and inspiration. As you write down the answers, write quickly without questioning or editing your thoughts. The examples after each question are some of the limiting beliefs that I used to have.

Take a couple of deep, cleansing breaths and relax. If it feels safe, close your eyes after each question and allow the answers to come forward, taking as much time as needed. Don't push yourself for an answer, just notice whatever thoughts pop up and write these down.

If you feel the urge to "be perfect," allow this thought to be one of your limiting beliefs and trust that whatever comes forward is the perfect thing for you right now.

Answer the following questions as thoroughly as you can:

What limiting beliefs do I have around my life?

Example: I am not capable of achieving my dreams, I don't belong, I am not worthy of living.

_____

_____

_____

What limiting beliefs do I have about myself?

Example: I am not good enough, I am not able to fall asleep, nobody wants to listen to what I am saying.

_____

_____

_____

What is stopping me from moving forward?

Example: Not believing in myself, not trusting myself, not feeling worthy of achieving my dreams.

_____

_____

_____

Who or what do I blame for my current situation?

Example: My first teacher, my classmates, myself for being so stupid.

_____

_____

_____

With awareness around your limiting beliefs, be as open and un-judgmental of yourself as you can. Know you are right now taking the next step forward in your healing process.

When you become aware of your limiting beliefs, the next step is to acknowledge them. By acknowledging you have these feelings, you let go of some of the pressure. As you acknowledge the limiting belief, you start the work of changing from the inside out.

Exercise 8: Acknowledge Your Current Situation

Now you are aware of one or more limiting beliefs, the next step is to answer the following questions.

Take a couple of deep cleansing breaths and relax. If it feels safe, close your eyes after each question and allow the answers to come forward taking as much time as needed. Do not close your eyes if you are driving or operating machinery. Don't push yourself for an answer, just notice whatever thoughts pop up and write these down.

Can I acknowledge myself right here and now with all the negative beliefs I have about myself, knowing that by acknowledging my situation I open up to move forward in my life?

_____

If the answer is "no" to the above question, ask yourself, "Would I rather be stuck in my current situation or would I rather move forward and release my internal blocks?"

_____

If you can't acknowledge yourself right now, remember it is a continual process. If you were my client, I would take you through an internal process to support you on a deeper level. For now, just relax in knowing that it is okay to feel stuck. Just continue reading and come back to this exercise later. As you progress through the book, you will find yourself more able to release your past step by step.

Acknowledging your current situation as best as you can right now will start eliminating your inner blocks. Know that **no matter whether you felt it or not,** the exercise you just did started an unconscious process enabling you to acknowledge and accept your current situation when you are ready to take the next step.

Note that some people find it easier to start acknowledging their limiting beliefs on a conscious level when they have experienced the tools that can help you deal with the internal blocks. We will come back to these tools later.

Congratulations on taking a significant step forward by doing these two exercises. I suggest you now sign the statement below to start embedding your newly gained insight on a deeper level.

If you couldn't do the exercise yet, commit to doing the exercise later by marking a specific time for it in your calendar.

Are you ready? Make the commitment to acknowledge yourself as you are right now, with your current challenges and limiting beliefs. With this, you are starting your healing process.

> *I am making the commitment that from this very moment*
> *I acknowledge myself and my challenges as thoroughly as*
> *I can. I know that up until now I have created my life to*
> *the best of my current abilities and that this is okay.*

Date: _____ *Name:* _____

Well done. I honor your commitment to move forward.

When You Feel You Don't Belong

I had gone to bed early on this weekend camp. Lying with my head turned towards the wall, I couldn't fall asleep. I felt insecure and alone. Suddenly giggling girls turned up beside the bed. They started to cover my hair with salt and pepper, whispering loudly about how stupid I was, how I deserved being alone, left out, and covered in salt and pepper. I lay on the bed pretending to sleep, afraid of what might happen if I stirred, with tears in my eyes and feeling worthless.

Have you ever experienced situations where you felt afraid and insecure and didn't know what to do or how to react the next day?

This and other situations had me feeling low, anxious, and insecure. I had all the symptoms of social anxiety; sneaking around along the walls, hiding in the kitchen as often as I could, pretending I was just offering my help. It was as if I experienced a lot of situations where I would feel tense and entirely not at peace with myself. I would see people whisper and think it was about me. I would notice a certain look my way and suddenly feel a rush of anxiety.

When you have experienced situations where you believe you are given the message, "you don't belong here," it is easy to start focusing on the negative. In my case, I started to focus on the message, "people don't want me."

This kind of focus is very unhealthy because whatever we focus on, we create more of. When you feel nervous, anxious and insecure, you are creating more of the same feelings. You might even reach the point where you have these feelings all the time.

What You Focus on Expands

Maybe you have heard about the Law of Attraction: *What we focus on, we attract more of.* Whether you believe there is a Law of Attraction or not, our mind takes in large amounts of information at any given time and selects a small subset to focus on. For example, when you walk into a room, even a big auditorium, your unconscious mind will take in everything. You can't consciously be aware of it all. Instead, you are aware of only a small fraction of all the things that are going on. And what you become aware of are the things that you focus on – consciously or subconsciously.

For example, imagine you are driving down a main road feeling hungry. What you focus on because of your rumbling stomach will be the restaurants and food stores. Suddenly your fuel lamp starts blinking, and you notice that if you don't find a gas station soon, you might not make it back home. Now you don't see the restaurants anymore; all you can focus on is finding the next gas station. Your unconscious mind is still noticing the restaurants and food stores, but quickly discarding them because something else is more important.

The critical insight here is that your brain is always selecting something to focus on. In the example above, that is helpful. But in some cases, your mind might have started focusing on negative things. That isn't helping you.

Now imagine you are walking into a room filled with people.

- First scenario: When you walk into this room feeling anxious, you will most likely notice the uninviting backs from people, their closed-up uninviting groups, someone laughing as they look your direction, etc. Your anxiety expands, and all you want to do is run away.

- Second scenario: Imagine you walk into the same room feeling secure and entirely at peace with yourself. Now you will most likely see the inviting person who looks at you with a smile. The groups that are open and inviting, the laughter shared among people in a positive way.

Which scenario do you want to experience?

You are not at the mercy of whatever your brain chooses to focus on. You can consciously direct your attention and focus to notice positive things that will help you.

Focus on the Mountaintop

Right now, you have a choice. You can keep focusing on the negative things, the things that don't work for you. Or you can focus on the possibilities. Start by paying attention to your thoughts.

Are you looking for a place to park your car, and don't believe there are any free parking places? Then your mind starts to focus on something else, and you are likely to miss the available options. On the other hand, if you say determinedly to yourself: "I know there is a parking place for me, and I am open to finding it," your mind will register any signs showing you a free place.

Do you have a car? Are you ever looking for a parking spot? Then I invite you to try this approach from now. Make a high-five with yourself every time it worked. Use these wins as a platform from where you can begin shifting how you perceive yourself and your abilities.

Maybe you believe you are stupid like I did. Whenever you notice you are letting yourself down, decide to restate this thought. Simply state to yourself, "I am smart." If this feels too much out of alignment with where you are now, choose the statement. "I am open to the possibility that I am smart."

What is it like for you to stand on the mountaintop? Imagine yourself standing on the top and feeling good about yourself. What do you believe you are capable of? How do you feel? What is the next step you can take to believe just a little more in yourself?

Right now, you might feel you have no clue and experience emotions rising up in you. This is totally fine. In the following sections, we are going to play with how we can move our emotions and create a better-feeling thought. And right after that, we will start to focus on your uniqueness. This is what makes your shine on your mountaintop.

This exercise helps you practice noticing your feelings in the moment. You then make a shift to a better thought. Read through the entire exercise first to get a sense of what you are going to do before you start.

Exercise 9: Notice How You Feel

This exercise is created to help you start becoming aware of what you are feeling in the moment. Do this exercise every day for a least a month and notice the change.

As you have practiced this exercise a couple of times, it will only take a few moments to get to a better place. The intention is not to shift from being totally depressed to totally happy. The purpose is to create a feeling one step better than the one you are feeling now.

1. I encourage you to start by setting a timer to go off several times doing your day. This could be every hour or whatever feels comfortable.

2. When the timer goes off: Stop whatever you are doing and notice what you are feeling.

3. Breathe through this feeling, and let it go, as best as you can, just for now.

4. Think about what you would rather feel. Envision that another you is standing right in front of you as if you are looking in a mirror. This other you is experiencing the better feeling. See yourself from the outside. You might sense your image is smiling and notice how it stands and how relaxed it is. Make this vision as clear and lifelike as you possibly can.

5. Now move into this image of you. Feel the feeling it is feeling, sense how your body posture changes. You might even notice a smile on your face.

6. Now, look at the situation you are currently in. From this new perspective, think of the next task you are about to do, and how you will do it from this new emotional state.

7. Well done. Now congratulate yourself for being open and aware and move on with your day.

This exercise is easier to learn as a guided practice. For your convenience, I have created an expanded, guided version of this exercise where I will guide you step by step through the process. You can download it from the book website www.lifeafterbullying.com.

Lotte's Tip

Practice the free guided version of this exercise a couple of times until it becomes natural for you. Most people listen to it 5 – 20 times and then occasionally, to refresh their memory. When you feel secure in the steps using the guided version, you can use the written version as a reminder of the steps.

After a while, you will start to notice your feelings more automatically. At this happens, you can stop using the timer.

You Are Capable of More Than You Think

We were a group of mothers supporting the Kindergarten making arts and crafts products to sell at a market. One lady was having difficulties creating a yarn hedgehog. The rest of the ladies, except me, were gathering around discussing how to make it. I have always been very creative and have made a lot of different arts and craft products throughout my life. Still, I held back, telling myself they would be just as capable as me in finding a solution. That there was nothing I could add that they wouldn't know. And especially, there was no reason for me to push forward acting like a "know-it-all."

Suddenly one of the ladies turned towards me and said, "Let's ask Mrs. Vesterli, she knows for sure."

This sentence, and the tone of voice, made a massive impact on me. Suddenly someone was telling me I could do something special. They expected me to find the solution. Combined with the fact that I had just decided I wouldn't interfere because they were as capable in figuring it out as I, this made me realize on a deeper level that I am unique. I started to acknowledge I was capable of something special. Not only creative things but in all walks of life.

We are all born unique with a special set of talents just for us. Being able to notice your uniqueness will help you move forward.

Recognize Your Talents

I was struggling, not believing in myself and too often pushing my accomplishments to the side without taking ownership of them. What I realized that day was that many of us are not aware of what we are good at. Because what we are good at usually comes naturally. Our talents seem so easy to use that we expect everyone else to be able to do the exact same things. We don't recognize our uniqueness and often fail to make the best use of it.

In Denmark where I live, we are often told not to show off. That doesn't work. We must be aware of our own power and what we are truly good at. This is not about putting yourself above other people. It's about knowing there are things you really are good at. You owe it to yourself to use these gifts to support yourself and other people. Everyone is good at different things. The best gift you can give to the world is to use your talents to do what you do best.

It is time to think about what you are good at. We are all unique, but often need to reflect a little to discover what our individual talents are. I have created an exercise that can help you notice your gifts and recognize your talents.

If you are writing in your journal, remember to set aside a couple of blank pages after you have completed the exercise to allow space to capture upcoming insights.

Exercise 10: Discovering Your Uniqueness

Make yourself comfortable. Read through the whole exercise before you start. Set aside at least half an hour of quiet time to do the first round. Relax by taking a few deep, slow, cleansing breaths and feel your body relax.

Start by becoming aware of the smaller and bigger things that you are good at. Think about the answers to the questions below and write the answers down. Write as quickly as you can, jotting down all your inspiration to stop yourself from judging your answers. Be aware this exercise is only starting the process. From this point forward, I invite you to keep writing whenever you notice things that you do well. This will give you a continually expanding list of skills and talents.

Question 1

Looking back, which situations stand out? For example, you got a compliment, someone said you made a difference with what you did, or you sensed it by the smile on their face.

_____

_____

_____

_____

Question 2

What things have you created that made you feel good or even proud of yourself when looking back? It can be things like doing repairs in your house, arts and craft projects (no matter how small), pictures taken, something written, or helping other people. Note that we are all different. Some people love to clean, others love cocking, and some love figuring out solutions to complex problems. In this exercise, there is no right or wrong answer – all that matters is that you stay true to yourself.

_____

_____

_____

_____

Question 3

Where did you make even a small difference in someone's life?

_____

_____

_____

_____

Question 4

From whom and for what have you gotten a compliment?

_____

_____

_____

_____

Question 5

If I were to ask your family, your friends, your neighbors, your schoolmates or coworkers about what makes you special – what answers would I get? Be honest and as best as you can, look at yourself from another perspective.

Be as honest as you possibly can. Keep writing as the answers rise in you and you become aware of them. Note that these questions are designed to open your mind to notice what you do well, and that the answers will keep rising to the surface. Keep noticing the answers as they show up and make sure to capture them in your journal, creating an, "I have accomplished this," list.

Doing this exercise, it might feel like you are bragging. That is correct. You are bragging – in a good way – to yourself so you can become truly aware of what you are capable of. This is important because it raises your core beliefs and supports you to feel better about yourself.

Well done. Acknowledging and honoring your skills helps you to grow your "belief" muscle and to find peace in yourself. Knowing what you do well opens you up for sharing your tools and talents. This allows you to support other people in different ways with your knowledge. Keep expanding the list and be open to acknowledging your own skills as you become aware of them.

Finding Peace in You

One day, I noticed myself sitting among a group of strangers sharing ideas, chatting and laughing, feeling totally relaxed. Wow. I hadn't even noticed I had come so far. A wave of peace flowed over me, making me take a deep breath and truly appreciate the situation and my relaxed feeling.

Using the steps described so far in this book, you are taking yourself to this inner peaceful feeling. Every time you feel relaxed, hopeful, and calm, notice it. Even if it is just for a few seconds, it is one step forward. You must open your awareness to all the small changes in and around you to support your journey.

The core concept of this book is to develop the peace in you. Most of the tools and exercises will support you in creating this inner peace. As you go through the book, keep noticing the changes you are going through, and the peace you feel. Write your observations, feelings, and progress in your journal.

Play Games and Find Peace

One thing I used to not even think about doing was to play. I used to be way too serious, not laughing out wholeheartedly, not remembering to play a game, to sing out loud or acting silly even when I was by myself.

Playing games with other people or just acting silly all by yourself allows you to relax from the inside out. Being fully present in what you are doing in the moment, having fun, is a great way to gain inner peace. It is about being able to put down your shield for a while and allow yourself to be you. Laughing out loud supporting the feeling of peace. Physical movements are especially healthy and can be the easiest games in the beginning. For many people being active automatically relaxes the body and makes it easier to be playful.

Play games with your kids or other children. It doesn't matter if you can't catch a ball, just make fun of it and praise the kid for how well they do. It is my experience that they don't care how good you are, as long as you can joke about it. And the funny thing is the more you joke, the more relaxed you get. I have found that making jokes, especially about myself, during a game relaxes me more and increases the fun.

In the beginning, you might find it easier to set aside your own protection when you are by yourself. This is totally fine. Try some of the ideas below to get out of your comfort zone safely and notice how you feel.

Ideas to playfully relax by yourself:

- Put on some uplifting rhythmic music and dance energetically, making all sorts of crazy movements. Put a big smile on your face even if it is forced to begin with. Even a forced smile sends signals to the mind that we are having fun. After just a few minutes of dancing, you will notice your mood changing. Crazy dancing and other movements work wonders when you can't get yourself started on a project or are feeling blue. It really does increase your energy.

- Brisk walking where you do some crazy steps occasionally works the same way.

- Singing inspiring songs is another way to uplift your spirit. It is vital that the music is inspiring and uplifting. Some music has negative lyrics or depressing rhymes and won't positively support you. Find something positive.

Set aside time every day, even if it is just 5 minutes, to do something playful that uplifts you. After a few weeks, you might find yourself hooked on this activity. If you have kids, find some games you can play together. Set the intention to play at least once a week or more often and make it a habit to joke about the result to create a fun, relaxed state. Remember this is not a competition, but all about having fun.

My kids are almost grown up and will soon leave home. It can be challenging to find time to play a game, but we still try to remember it regularly. And at least once a month we make sure to do some activities outside the house where we can enjoy ourselves fully. This can be anything – seeing a movie or play, visiting a museum or going out for dinner. What is your situation? And how can you create more time to have fun in your life? Think about it and make a list in your journal.

Lotte's Tip

Brainstorm things that raise your level of joy. What things make you relax, laugh, and feel playful? Make a list of your answers and hang it somewhere you will see it regularly. Whenever you feel low, stressed or anxious, look at your list and see what you can do right now to uplift your spirit. Do it and feel the difference.

It can be helpful to divide the list by how time-consuming the different ideas are. Example categories could be "less than 5 minutes," "less than half an hour" or "more than half an hour." For example, one thing that really relaxes me is doing something creative with my hands, especially something that will have me fully concentrated. This is relatively time-consuming, and when I don't have a least an hour, I can't relax fully into it. Going for a walk is another thing that I benefit from. This is more flexible and can be anything from 10 minutes up to several hours. When I only have 5 minutes or less and need a boost, I often put on some rhythmic, inspiring music and do some crazy dancing.

If you don't have time right now to create your list, set aside time in your calendar to create it as soon as possible. Write your list so there is room to add more ideas as you come up with them.

Summary

Finding peace in you is a step-by-step process. You have started the process of accepting yourself. Even if you have just started this process, and still feel there is much work to do before you can accept yourself fully, you have opened up for the internal healing process to start.

Becoming aware of your emotions supports you in accepting and consciously creating a better feeling. And in the process of relaxing in your own skin, you free up the energy you previously spent showing a façade to the world where you pretended that everything was okay.

What you focus on expands. Being aware of your thinking supports you in looking out for the things you want to have more of. Whenever you become aware of your own thinking, you can make a shift to a better feeling.

Take ownership of your life and accept that you are good at something, and probably more than you are currently aware of. Own it and start using your uniqueness for the benefit of yourself and others.

Create a playful life by taking just 5 minutes a day to get into the habit of playing and laughing. Look for playfulness in any situation and use it feel more relaxed and joyful.

The next step is to look at how you can free yourself and continue the process to love yourself on a deeper level.

Lotte's Strategies to Increase Your Quality of Life

- ✔ Take ownership of your life.

- ✔ Your uniqueness defines you – uncover your talents.

- ✔ Know what brings you joy and make time to add in a little each day.

- ✔ Be aware of your thoughts and make a habit of changing them from limiting to empowering.

- ✔ Trust you are a capable, strong, and powerful human being, that you are truly worthy of living a wonderful, inspiring life.

Chapter 4

Finding Your Voice

"I've finally stopped running away from myself. Who else is there better to be?"

GOLDIE HAWN

Get Comfortable with Your Voice

*"I can't hear you. **Speak up.**"*

I was embarrassed as I got special permission in high school to work with a speech therapist. My voice had become a big problem. It sounded like a whisper, and my mumbling made it even worse. It had come to the point where most people lost interest in listening to me, interrupting and speaking over me as though they hadn't heard me. In all fairness, they probably hadn't. But it felt like I was always being interrupted, was never heard, and not taken seriously.

The more insecure I felt in a situation, the quieter I became. Class situations, where I used to be bullied, were terrible. In social situations, my lack of voice was also impeding me. The more people spoke up without listening to me, the more insecure I would become. Before long, I would just sit quietly in a corner, pretending to listen to a conversation and feeling bad about myself.

How Comfortable Are You with Your Voice?

How is your voice today? Do you feel like you have lost your voice? Have trouble speaking up? Being heard?

I know most of you do feel anxious about speaking because I have heard this repeatedly from my clients. Anxiety around speaking can appear in any situation from public speaking in front of large audiences to speaking to just one other person. No matter what level of anxiety you feel around speaking up, freeing up your voice is entirely possible.

To get comfortable raising your voice and learning to speak clearly again is a process like any new habit. The more secure you become, and the more consciously aware of your voice you are, the easier it becomes. To get comfortable with your voice involves moving your comfort zone little by little to free up your voice. It is gratifying to be able to be heard, and it allows you to have a positive impact on the lives of those around you.

Freeing Up Your Voice

Working with the speech therapist improved my voice some. "Start your voice from your belly. Articulate clearly. Turn up your volume." My speech therapist went on and on with exercises, do's and don'ts. Great tools that were very useful, except for one missing link.

The Missing Link

The challenge was that even though I could speak up in front of my speech therapist, it was still a struggle to speak up and use the tools I had learned outside his office. He focused on the techniques, but what was missing was an improvement of my self-esteem. Without an inner trust, I was not able to open my mouth and speak loudly and freely in front of other people.

There is no doubt that learning these techniques has been helpful for me. As I grew my self-esteem and inner worth, I started to be able to use them to improve my speech. Today I speak in front of hundreds of people and am no longer afraid of speaking up and sharing my message. I appreciate this dramatic change daily and am often reminded of it when I teach people to free their voice and stand up for themselves.

Through my own recovery journey, I realized my self-development work supported me in freeing my voice. As I grew personally, I integrated the exercises and techniques I learned from speech therapists and speaker training. While I was losing my voice, I had started to mumble and wasn't using my body to support my voice at all. There were many techniques I had to integrate to be able to speak clearly again. But I could not start without loving myself.

Working with your voice both from the inside and outside supports you in freeing your voice with more ease. From the inside, you need to release your inner blocks and improve your self-esteem. From the outside, you can use specific voice training exercises. Doing both at the same time will make you able to speak louder and with more ease.

Lotte's Tip

One easy way to get some voice training is to join a choir. The warm-up exercises they do for their voices are great for training your voice at home too.

Place Your Voice

A simple tool you can train at home and use as you get more comfortable with yourself is to place your voice correctly.

Where are you placing your voice when you speak? Placing your voice at the wall at the end of the room is good when you speak to a crowd of people. Speaking to one person, you place your voice just behind this person as if there was a wall just behind him/her.

When you have anxiety and low self-worth, you tend to place your voice just in front of yourself, fading away before it even reaches the other person.

One great exercise you can use right now is to focus on where you place your voice. Many people who have lost their voice due to lack of self-esteem place their voice very close to themselves. This causes it to only be audible from a very short distance.

Practicing placing your voice further out is very helpful. The great thing is that you can practice this technique at home – training your voice externally as you grow internally. Use this exercise to rehearse if you need to speak in front of a group or use it merely to level up your voice.

Exercise 11: Placing Your Voice

Please read through the entire exercise through before you start.

1. Stand at one end of the room.

2. At the other end, place an empty chair facing you. Now imagine someone sitting in the chair. This can be a person you want to communicate something to, for example, a participant in a meeting or a group of people you are giving a presentation to.

3. Facing the chair, speak out as loudly as you can. Speak slowly and deliberately and articulate to the point where it seems as if you are making fun of someone. Be as clear as you possibly can and practice the words you want to say in the situation that you are visualizing.

4. If you can: Tighten your stomach and breathe slowly and deeply. This can support you to add volume to your words.

5. Sense your words reaching out to the other end of the room by focusing on the chair or even better, a point behind the chair.

6. As you speak slowly and as clearly as you possibly can, feel your voice reach the other end of the room.

Tip: This exercise works best when you know that you are home alone. Especially until you get more comfortable with it.

Take small steps to raise your voice and notice how it feels to stand up and speak your truth even when you have butterflies in your stomach. Remember to go easy and congratulate yourself every time you have either practiced at home or spoken to one or more people.

Lotte's Tip

Get into the habit of practicing your voice whenever you have the opportunity. In the beginning, it might be easier to practice when you are among strangers. For example, speak louder and articulate more to the sales assistant. Little by little, you shift your comfort zone and can speak louder in every situation.

Love Yourself and Raise Your Voice

I was having lunch with a group of friends. As I asked for a piece of cucumber, I swallowed the first syllable, and only the word "cumber" came out of my mouth. Everybody laughed.

I had started to develop speech problems due to my low self-esteem. My voice had become very low, and I had even begun to struggle with pronouncing some words every now and then. Sometimes people would laugh when I struggled to say what I wanted, and it would pierce my heart. I would get quieter, feel even more stupid, and hate myself and my inability to speak clearly.

How Do You Feel About Yourself?

When you feel stupid, unworthy, and hate yourself, you drain yourself. I didn't believe anyone could love me as I didn't love myself.

How are you feeling about yourself today? Are you on a downward spiral where you believe you are no good and are finding evidence to support that belief all around you? Doesn't that feel like a place you don't want to be anymore?

Learning to Love Myself

As I moved forward in my self-development journey, I was told that I had to love myself to heal. In the beginning, I thought that was ridiculous for two main reasons: First, I couldn't love myself because of all the negative beliefs embedded in my body. Second, I believed that focusing on myself would be to raise myself above others and was a selfish and self-centered thing to do.

One day I realized that when I placed a lot of blame, guilt, and self-hatred on myself, I couldn't give the love and care to my family that I wanted to. That thought went right to my heart: to give love, you have to be love. To be love, you must own, care for, and love yourself. And every little shift you experience makes you able to give a little more love to your family and to everyone else.

If you don't love yourself and take care of yourself first, it is tough to give true love and care for others. Self-love and self-care are about being true to yourself first to be true to others.

This is entirely different from being selfish or self-centered. Selfishness is focusing solely on yourself without thinking of other people, and self-centeredness means that nobody else counts. Self-love and self-care is the opposite of this and is what we need to aspire to.

Your Accomplishments Start from Within

How can you accomplish anything if you don't love yourself? Trust yourself? Believe in yourself? And have a feeling that your voice matters?

More importantly, how can anybody love you when you don't love yourself?

I was lucky as I found a boyfriend who was able to look behind my shield and see the person I was. He supported me through my journey. Today we have been married for more than 20 years. But to be honest, our love escalated when I was able to start loving myself because that meant I could be more open and free around my husband.

Today we sit back every New Year's Eve and look back at the past year and talk about how our love is more profound than ever before. I have no doubt that it is mostly because of my personal journey. And I am not alone feeling this way. Several clients have come back with stories about improved family relationships both with their spouses and kids as they started to truly love themselves.

Loving yourself gives you freedom and inner confidence. People want to get to know you because you radiate an inner power. This is especially true when you have been deeply hurt in your past. When you go through the healing stages, you grow from your experience. Your inner soul becomes deep and powerful and will feel supportive and interesting to other people.

Look around the world of transformational leaders today. The most powerful people have all been deeply hurt or gone through tough issues in their past. They have been able to take a deep breath in, work on themselves, and move forward. Now they are inspiring other people to do the same. It is your turn to make a turnaround, to set yourself free, and to love yourself from within.

The Journey to Love Yourself

As with everything else, being able to love yourself is a journey. You will be changing little by little as you do the exercises.

One of the most profound exercises I have come across is the **mirror exercise**. This is a short exercise designed to be used daily just before going to bed. The mirror exercise seems simple, and yet it is very powerful. I have had many clients come back to me after practicing this exercise for a few weeks and tell me how it is changing their life.

Here are some examples of what my clients have said about their experience:

- "I started to cry and could hardly finish the first time. Then I experienced a remarkable relief."

- "I came out from a meeting and realized I was mentally patting myself on the back acknowledging myself for the job I did."

- "In the beginning, I couldn't do it looking in the mirror, so I would lie in my bed every evening doing the exercise before I went to sleep. Slowly I started to recognize the bright colors and the good things in my life."

Now it's your turn. Make the mirror exercise a daily habit. I recommend you do it every day for at least **40 days in a row**. After the first 40 days, you can pass every now and then, but I still recommend you keep the mirror exercise as a daily habit. Over time, you will realize the changes taking place deep within.

Exercise 12: Mirror Exercise

The mirror exercise is about acknowledging yourself, recognizing the power in you and opening up to loving yourself on a deep level.

Do the mirror exercise in a private place. This can be in the bathroom, as you get ready to go to bed. Lock the door so that you won't be disturbed. You want privacy to give yourself permission to play full out.

Look your reflection in the eyes and state what you would want to say as if you are a loving person speaking to you. Keep eye-contact throughout the whole exercise.

Repeat the following sentences at least three times each completing them using new things every time. And start every sentence by saying your name:

"Name" I love that you …

"Name" I am proud that you …

"Name" I forgive you for …

"Name" I am committed to …

Note that you can complete the sentences the same way every day if you want. They just need to be 3 or more different things on the current day. Over time you will start realizing new things you can complete the sentence with.

The last – crucial - step to this exercise is this:

Look yourself in the eye and hold your gaze for at least 30 seconds as you say out loud: "name, I love you." Remember to keep looking in your eyes as you say it and to keep breathing slowly and deeply.

Note that this last step very often brings tears to your eyes and can stir up a lot of feelings. This is totally fine and part of the healing taking place.

In the beginning, you might be using small things to complete the sentences. Like "Lotte, I am proud that you noticed that the grass is green today," or, "Lotte, I forgive you for eating that extra cookie today," This is totally fine. As you get more into the exercise, you will want to go deeper.

Some of my sentences over the years have been

- "Lotte, I forgive you for blaming your teacher and feeling a victim for so many years."

- "Lotte, I forgive you for comfort eating even though you know that you feel bad afterward."

- "Lotte, I am proud you spoke up to your teacher about changing the schedule."

An everyday evening with the mirror exercise for me can sound like this:

- Lotte, I love you for playing a game with your kids.

- Lotte, I love your smile.

- Lotte, I love the look of the muscles in your arms.

- Lotte, I am proud you got through all of today's emails.

- Lotte, I am proud you did the phone call you had been putting off.

- Lotte, I am proud you went out for a walk even though it rained.

- Lotte, I forgive you for not focusing on writing on your book today.

- Lotte, I forgive you for eating that extra cookie.

- Lotte, I forgive you for not speaking up at the meeting.

- Lotte, I am committed to adhering to my fasting day tomorrow.

- Lotte, I am committed to raising my hand with the purpose of asking at least one question at the training tomorrow.

- Lotte, I am committed to writing for a minimum of one hour on my book tomorrow.

- Lotte, I love you.

When you can love yourself, you can stand up for your own. You stop caring so much about what other people say because you know yourself best. It gets easier to put your foot down and say "No." And it gets easier to speak up for yourself and for others. When you love yourself, you free your voice.

Lotte's Tip

Loving yourself also means taking care of yourself. Take care of yourself first to give yourself time to rest and recharge your batteries. Start listening to your inner voice to hear your internal feedback whenever you are asked to do anything. Stay true to your internal voice and say it out loud if there is something you don't want. To say "No" to things you don't want to do and to the things that you honestly do not have time for.

Saying "No" is one of the greatest gifts we can give ourselves in this speeding world. Because if you don't allow time to be you, you have nothing to give to others. Eventually, you will end up depressed and stressed.

Saying "No" is one of the things that many of my clients find challenging. I even find it challenging myself. The more we know of our purpose and goals, the more aware we become of when to say no. In Part Three, I will guide you through an exercise that will support you in realizing when and how to say "No." Right now, just be aware that if you feel like saying "No" it is most likely the best thing you can do, and by saying "No" you are honoring yourself.

Summary

In this chapter, the focus has been on our voice, as our voice resonates with our feelings. When we feel low, the risk of losing our voice is acute. You have learned several ways to train your voice. You have also gotten the knowledge that the exercises in this book will support you in raising your voice.

An important aspect of freeing up your voice is to love yourself despite your past and current challenges. When you love yourself, it is possible to let go of other reactions more easily when we notice them. Crucially, when you love yourself, you can open up to loving other people more deeply and openly. As you start being more aware of your own reactions and feelings, you are opening up to healing your past.

One of the best exercises to learn to love yourself is the mirror exercise. Committing yourself to go through the mirror exercise every evening, starting with 40 days in a row, is one of the best steps you can do for yourself right now. Start right now – tonight – and move forward with your healing. I truly honor you for taking this step. You are worthy of healing your past, of loving yourself, and of moving forward and raising your voice.

Lotte's Strategies to Increase Your Quality of Life

- ✔ Free your voice by consistently working on loving yourself.

- ✔ Loving yourself starts today. You will increase your love of yourself as you do the different exercises.

- ✔ Do the mirror exercise for 40 days in a row to get you started.

Moving on to the Next Part of Your Journey

Wouldn't it be nice to have a magic wand that could propel us forward to a life where we truly love ourselves, feel comfortable, and are at peace? Of course, this isn't possible and honestly isn't even desirable. Yes, I would have loved to be propelled to the place I am today or even further ahead. Yet I value the wisdom and power I have gained from my experience throughout the journey to heal from my past.

When you change and grow your life at your own pace, you learn to be the changed you. You learn new habits and new ways to react when challenges show up. You learn to regain your inner peace and decrease your stress level.

You have taken the first step to your recovery. You have learned to acknowledge who you are, listed the skills and knowledge that you have, and have started to own yourself and your inner power.

Now it's time to move forward and take the next step. In Part Two, you will look at where you want to go. What do you want to accomplish and what will your life look like when you have gained your inner power?

Next, you will lay out the roadmap for your success. When you have a picture in your mind of where you want to go, it is easier to take the right steps and blast through the challenges that show up along the way.

Part Two

Creating Your
Blueprint for Success

Chapter 5

Create the Future That's Fulfilling for You

"To know what you want is the first step in the journey of life."

WAEL EL-MANZALAWY

Starting the Process

I felt as though I was walking through a forest not having any clear direction. Up until now, I had just been following the flow, and I was fed up with being the old me. It was time to change, time to be more aware of what I wanted, time to live the life I desired.

I knew by now, having gone through the steps in Part One of this book, that I was worthy and capable of making changes in my life. I didn't know how far I could go, but I realized that every little step would make my life easier and more enjoyable.

My big question was where to start. I figured out that instead of just walking randomly around, doing a little here and there, it was essential to have a goal. This led me to think about what my life could look like when I turned it around, and I asked myself questions like:

- What do I want?

- What does my ideal life look like?

- When do I forget time and place doing things that I love?

- What gives my life value?

Creating Your New Life

The answers developed as I spent time thinking about the questions and I keep going through these exercises at least once every year. As I keep improving myself, new things come in, and old things change or drop out. Going through the exercises every year creates my ongoing blueprint for success.

If you wanted to build a new home, you wouldn't just pick a place randomly and start building the house from whatever materials you could find lying around. So why would you treat your life in this way? You want to have a clear idea of where you are heading. You want to look at your destination from where you are today.

You deserve to take the time to create your inner blueprint and lay the foundation for success.

I will guide you through the steps to create your blueprint for success. First, we will dive into the foundation of a great goal. We will examine how you can own your goal to increase your chance of achieving it. And we will investigate what is truly meaningful for you, what you are passionate about, and what adds value to your life.

In Chapter Six, you will learn how to set good, achievable goals. I invite you to go through the progress to set your own goals. Chapter Seven considers how to achieve your goals once you have created them.

Turning Your Life Around

You need two things to turn your life around: a strong desire and a clear blueprint. It is totally fine that you might not know exactly how to create the change yet, as long as you have the desire to do it. I will help you create your blueprint for success to make the change you desire. The more you work on these steps, the more clarity you get.

Remember your internal belief of what you are capable of is likely to change as you grow. I recommend you evaluate your goals and what gives your life meaning at least once a year.

Goal setting is like setting up your inner GPS. You might not have a clear picture of the entire route to your goal, and you don't need to know at this moment. Being clear on where you want to go is the key to get there as quickly and easily as possible. You avoid spending time jumping around between techniques, trying one thing here and another there, and not really getting anywhere.

The best way to create your blueprint for success is by going through the exercises step by step. The more time you spend on these steps, the clearer an answer you will get and the easier the journey will be. It is worth taking your time on this part of the journey. Even if you don't have time today, make sure to schedule time as soon as possible to do the exercises.

The foundation of a great goal is to own the goal fully. And this is precisely what we are going to focus on next.

Owning Your Goal

Eric smoked. Despite the fact he was working in health care, he still smoked. He had tried quitting several times but to no avail. He knew it would be beneficial for his health and overall well-being to quit.

The challenge was that it wasn't a goal he truly wanted to achieve in his heart. Smoking felt calming and relaxing in his busy life. To quit smoking was therefore mainly an "I should" goal created by other people and society.

An "I should" goal is tough to achieve. It requires a strong will. Even if you do achieve it, there is little chance the results will last. "Should" goals come in many forms. Some of the common goals that you have probably either had yourself or know someone who has had are:

- Weight-loss goals. You lose weight and then gain it back right after you have achieved your goal – if you ever achieve it.

- Quit smoking goals. You might stop, and then start soon after when you attend an event with your friends who still smoke.

- Exercise goals. You start exercising and by pure willpower drag yourself through the event you signed up for – and then immediately quit exercising again.

I am sure you know where you have been challenged by your goals.

Know that "should" goals are very common. Be aware of your motivation and from now on only set goals you truly want to achieve. Or find a way to transform a "should" goal into an, "I want this," goal.

Creating the Shift

The big realization came to Eric one day where he was out running his usual route around the lake. He enjoyed taking in the nice fresh air and was feeling great. Coming back, he automatically reached for a cigarette, lit it and started inhaling. Then he realized how ridiculous it was. "I just ran around the lake," he thought, "filling my lungs with the wonderful fresh, clean air, and now I pollute them again and lose the benefits I just got."

At that moment, he managed to transfer his knowledge about smoking to his heart level and decided to stop. When he told me the story, he hadn't smoked for several years. The decision to stop was so strong that it made it easy to stick to, even when it wasn't easy to go through the body's reactions from not getting the drug.

You have probably set many goals throughout your life. A great deal of these will have been "should" goals, or goals that were things you would like to achieve but didn't really, sincerely desire. When you don't truly own your goal at the heart level, it is harder to achieve. And if you reach the goal, the goal state is much harder to maintain. Goals like this are overwhelmingly likely to fail.

When Your Goal Makes You Reach for the Mountaintop

Great goals are things you genuinely want, things you have a high desire to accomplish, and that are meaningful to you. These are powerful goals that make you reach for the mountaintop and have a fair chance of being achieved. Truly wanting your goals makes it easier to endure the challenges of achieving them.

I invite you to start collecting inspiration for goals in your diary. Set aside a couple of pages reserved for capturing your ideas. Don't worry about stating a clear goal. I will guide you through clarifying your goal in the next chapter. For now, you just want to capture your inspiration. Whenever you think of something, ask yourself: "is this a goal I truly want? Or is it a 'should' goal?"

Do You Really Need Your Goal?

When your goal isn't really your *own* goal, the risk is that you will hover at the base of the mountain, moving up one hill and down the next, never reaching the top. When you realize that your goal is an "I should" goal, it is time to reconsider.

There are two main categories of "I should" goals.

- Either they are things you think you "should" do because other people do it and want you to do the same. In this case, be willing to say "No." Stay true to yourself and only work on goals you genuinely want to have as well.

- Or they are things you know will make you feel better, but they are formulated by someone else. In this case, it is worth working on the *why* behind the goal. The why behind the goal is often the benefits you will get when you have achieved your goal.

Work on your goal until you can make it an "I want this" goal. For instance, if you have a weight-loss goal, it might be because you want to be able to run and play with your kids more easily. Or you might want to be able to walk without feeling the pain in your knees from carrying around too much weight. Both can be things that you want to create. Then the goal is to be able to walk freely for half an hour, and the way to reach your goal, in this case, is by losing weight.

Think about the real benefit from achieving your goals and let this support you in making your goal a genuine "I want this" goal. The ideal state is to have a goal that you want to achieve no matter what.

A Note on Comforting Habits

When you are experiencing low self-esteem, anxiety, and other negative emotions, it is common to suffer from addictions like smoking, drinking, or overeating, because it calms our nerves.

When I was young, I would eat for comfort. It helped in the moment, but it never felt good afterward. Despite my intellectual knowledge, I would comfort eat anyway when I felt unworthy and bad about myself.

Whatever challenges you have, know that it is possible to achieve your goal when you genuinely want it and you use the tools in this book. When you start to feel better about yourself, it will be easier to get rid of old habits.

Adding Meaning to Your Life

I felt tired, stressed, and not very good about myself. When I came home from work, I would take care of my kids, cook dinner, do the household chores, and never take care of myself. I love my family, and they have always been my priority.

Then I realized there was one thing that was even more important – and if I did this one thing, I could actually be a better mom. Doing this one thing keeps me fueled and increases my ability to bounce back and be more present with my family.

The first time I went through a process to find out what gave my life meaning, I was surprised that walking in nature was my number one priority. Even over doing activities with my kids. I couldn't wrap my head around it – it didn't feel right. For me, being a mom, cooking healthy meals, and playing with my kids was important.

Then I realized that when I didn't get outside and didn't take time for me to just be in nature and walk or run for half an hour, I would be uptight, more easily stressed, and have less energy. That was very surprising. I thought about all those times I had stopped myself going out into nature. Just because I felt that I "should" concentrate on the work at home and be with my kids.

As I started to take time to walk every day, I became calmer, had more energy, and was able to fully enjoy being with my kids. And they got a more easy-going mom with more energy. Following what was giving my life value and taking time to be in nature was beneficial for my kids, my work, and my everyday life.

Use the Right Fuel for Your Engine

Being true to what is meaningful for you is like using the right fuel to run your engine. Discovering what is meaningful – your inner values – helps you be more present and gives you the energy to focus on tasks. And it makes everything you do more fun.

If tasty food gives your life meaning, then going on a strict, boring diet can really be draining. Instead, mindful eating can be a better solution.

You might have lost track of what gives your life meaning, what you used to love to do. Or you might not do it now, because you are not allowing yourself the time. As you become aware of the things that give your life meaning, you will also become aware of how vital they are for your well-being.

It is easier to go after a goal that is aligned with what gives your life meaning, your passions, and inner values. For example, if you want to work on your social anxiety, enrolling in a class to reconnect with something that you used to love, but haven't allowed yourself to do for a long time, makes it easier to come out among other people.

The Treasure Hunt

Discovering the inner values that give your life meaning is a step-by-step process. Today, you might have closed internal doors to some of your values. Maybe someone teased you about the things you loved to do, or there are things that you believe should come first. I felt that way about work and keeping the house.

Right now, I will guide you through an exercise that is created to support you in rediscovering your values and personal treasures. Be open to doing this exercise again – there might be changes as you develop yourself, and as you transition different phases in life. You can do this exercise once a year as part as setting your goals for the next year.

> **Lotte's Tip**
>
> When you do the exercise, be open to following your intuition. The more you write down the first words that pop up in your head, the more you stay true to your core. You might come up with things that are not on your radar right now. This is totally fine and can give you great awareness of your real desire.

Exercise 13: Find Meaning in Your Life

Set aside at least half an hour of undisturbed time. Turn off your phone and other notifications. If you don't have time right now, schedule a time in your calendar to do this exercise. Read through the entire exercise before starting.

When you do the exercise, be as open as possible to your inner voice. Don't evaluate what comes forward but write down uncensored any inspiration you get.

Exercise: Finding Meaning in My Life - Step One

Answering the following questions supports you in discovering where you can add more meaning to your life.

Answer each question like this: Close your eyes. Take three deep, calming breaths inhaling all the way and exhaling all the way to your stomach.

Set the intention to be open to discovering what it is that gives your life meaning. Now open your eyes and begin answering the questions below. Write as fast as you can to bypass your conscious mind and go deeper into your core. The point here is to get as many keywords down as possible.

You are welcome to repeat your answers in the different questions.

What is it that creates the most meaning for you when you do it?

_____

_____

What gives you most joy?

_____

_____

What do you do when you feel most fulfilled?

_____

_____

What do you do when you completely forget time?

_____

_____

What did you love to do as a child but never find the time to do anymore? (Maybe someone teased you and you stopped?)

_____

_____

If you would get paid to do anything at all – what would you be doing?

_____

_____

When you are most tense, what do you do to calm yourself that feels good afterwards?

_____

_____

What do you long to do, but never act on?

_____

_____

What do you do that gives you more energy?

_____

_____

Well done. By now, you might have a lot of things that add meaning to your life. Now you want to find the few things to act on now.

Exercise: Finding Meaning in My Life - Step Two

Look at your list of things. What stands out for you? Which items are the ones you most want to act on? It can be something you haven't given yourself time to do – or something you have always longed to learn.

Use a bright colored marker to highlight the items that stand out for you. Aim to highlight between one and five things that are most important for you right now.

You might feel bad you haven't allowed these core values to be part of your life. That's okay. Know that you have started listening to what is most necessary for you to grow and thrive. Slowly, you are taking steps to live your own life. Over the next couple of months, you will most likely start feeling a significant change in your life as you begin to listen to your own inner wisdom. Remember, this is a continual process, and it is okay to go easy on yourself.

Creating a Starting Point

Looking at your list, consider how much you are currently implementing the things that add meaning to your life. Also, think about specific things you can do today to add more of this into your life.

When I realized that going for a walk in nature was one of my core values, I hardly ever allowed myself to go for a walk. The action step I took was to buy a pedometer so that I could track how many steps I took. This helped me allow myself to take a walk even though I had many other tasks that felt "more urgent." Later, when I felt the benefits, it was easy for me to go for a walk just because I "felt the need."

Now it is your turn to act on your values and start adding more meaning to your life.

Exercise: Finding Meaning in My Life – Step Three

Choose one highlighted thing from your list – one of the values that give your life more meaning

_____

How you would feel if you could do more of this regularly?

_____

What is one specific step you could take today to start implementing this on a daily or weekly basis?

_____

Decide on a specific time and date to start within the coming week:

_____

Now you know what creates meaning in your life and what is valuable to you, it's time to move forward to create your goals. When you are aligned with your core values, it is much easier to create an "I want this" goal. You will discover this as you continue doing the work.

Summary

You have started the process of creating your blueprint for success. You have learned what often stops us from achieving our goals – the critical difference between an "I should" goal and an "I want this" goal. You have also worked on discovering your core values, the things that add meaning to your life. Remember you can do the value exercise regularly as you develop and grow.

Lotte's Strategies to Increase Your Quality of Life:

- ✔ Take time to think about what you really desire.

- ✔ Get into the habit of carrying a notebook to jot down any inspiration you get.

- ✔ Take time to find the right fuel for your engine: What gives your life meaning? What do you value most in your life?

Chapter 6

Creating Your Goal

"Setting goals is the first step in turning the invisible into the visible."

TONY ROBBINS

The First Draft

I was sitting in a crowd, participating in a "create your dream" visualization. A vision came up, and I saw myself turning into an eagle flying high over the countryside, over the mountains, and over the oceans. And as I flew, I saw myself speaking in various places around the world.

For me, this felt like a terrifying vision. I had only just started to develop my voice. I simply couldn't see myself standing in front of people. Especially not in front of the size of crowd I saw in the vision.

The vision was clear enough to make the tears stream down my face. As I went to speak with one of the supporters, I was only a little comforted by his words: "You only get a dream that you are actually able to accomplish."

That was hard to believe with the way I felt at the time. I just could not see myself being comfortable speaking to any size crowd. I was uncomfortable just going up to people to start a conversation, and yet the vision had been very clear.

Since then I have had many small and bigger goals around speaking up. From one-on-one conversations up to large speaking engagements. Today, I have spoken in front of more than 100 people multiple times. I still have my vision coming up in my meditations from time to time. Now, I feel comfortable and eager to speak in the various places I envision.

The Power of Dreaming

Setting goals is essential. Without a clear picture of your destination, it is difficult to take the right actions. And it is hard to measure your progress.

Yet too often, people set the wrong goals. Either they set goals they don't truly desire or goals stated in a way that doesn't set their minds to work towards the desired outcome. A great goal is a goal you genuinely want, which is aligned with your core values and is stated so that you can measure the result.

The first step to a great goal is to do some internal research. Let's say you want to build a house. First, you would spend time looking for the right place to build and the right type of house. This is what I call the dreaming phase of goal-setting.

Without allowing yourself to dream, how can you expand yourself? Life is not about living someone else dream, it is about you and what *you* desire.

It is time to dream. Set aside an hour and find a place where you can be totally undisturbed. If you can't do this right now, select a time when you will do this process and schedule it in your calendar. Doing this exercise gives you directions and fuel to keep moving.

The Dream Phases

As you access the dreaming phase, be open to big dreams. It doesn't matter if you don't know how you can accomplish your dream. This will show up as your life expands. Your dream will probably feel outside your comfort zone. This is because if you stay in the same place without taking new steps, your life will remain the same. Walt Disney said: "If you can dream it, you can do it." It took him many years to create Disney Studios, and he had a lot of setbacks on the journey. He kept pursuing his dream, and we all know where that led him.

As you dream, you can use information from people you know and movies you have seen. This is not cheating - you are assembling a vision from every source of inspiration and knowledge you have.

As you go through the following exercise, don't limit yourself by your current life situation. A dream can be small and tangible, or it can be big and almost incomprehensible. I had a huge vision with no clue about how to achieve it. The exercise allows you to open up for your dreams, no matter what size.

If this is the first time you open up to dreaming about your goals, you might find that you are seeing only a few small goals that you can reach over the next year. This is totally fine. As you develop and grow, you will build trust in yourself. And when you continue to dream on a regular basis, you will experience that your dreams get bigger and bigger.

Do this exercise today and continue to do it at least once a year. I usually do it around New Year in preparation for the year to come.

As you do the exercise, let go of any expectations or judgment towards yourself. Just relax and enjoy the process and know that whatever you receive is fine.

Most people find it beneficial to do the exercise with their eyes closed, having someone read the questions out loud. This makes it easier to go deep within. For your benefit, I have created a free guided version of this exercise you can download from my website.

Exercise 14: Dream

Read through the whole exercise before starting the process.

Set yourself up for dreaming. This can be by placing yourself in a comfortable chair in a quiet place, putting on some nice relaxing music, and maybe lighting a candle. You can also find a beautiful, restful place in nature. Make sure you have pen and paper ready in front of you to capture your thoughts. And remember to put your phone in flight mode and turn off any notifications.

Take a deep breath in, exhale, and let go of any tension in your body. Breathe deeply and slowly in and out three more times.

Now visualize being at the ideal place and time in your future life.

What does your ideal life look like?

_____

Where are you living?

_____

With whom are you living?

_____

What do your surroundings look like?

_____

How are you dressed?

_____

How are you interacting with other people – family, friends, coworkers, and strangers?

_____

What are you doing with your life?

_____

What have you been doing over the past year to get to this point?

_____

Be open to capturing any thoughts that go through your mind. This is your inspiration that becomes the raw material for creating your goals.

Your thoughts represent your feelings and your wishes for the future. Some of these thoughts will be positive images and inspiration for you.

Other thoughts might be limiting beliefs. You might tell yourself, "I can't do this." "I'm not good enough." "Who am I to dream this big?" These limiting thoughts guide you to areas of your life that you want to change.

Make a note of all these limiting thoughts. In Part Three, I will teach you tools and ways to work with these limiting beliefs that you can use on an ongoing basis. Make it a habit to make a note of any self-limiting belief as they come up.

Note that your dream might very well be scary to you. Mine was in the beginning, but now I have learned to trust it. We cannot dream a goal we are not capable of achieving. Dreaming is the first step to setting goals.

Paint your future as best as you can right now. Know that you can keep coming back as you grow and expand. You can keep changing it, adding more details, more colors, etc. Write your dream down as fully as possible. If you are a visual kind of person, you might even want to draw it.

Know What You Want

With this dream in place, it is time for you to create your wish list. Look at your notes and start writing down your wishes. Answer the question "What do I want?" Don't limit yourself to your description of your dream but write down everything that comes to mind. The longer you do this exercise, the deeper you get into your core wishes for your life.

Some of your wishes are likely to be aligned with what will make your life meaningful. Or they can relate to what your life can be like when you start trusting your own abilities. Be open and allow yourself to follow your intuition without evaluating.

Exercise 15: Create a List of Your Deepest Wishes

Find a quiet place. Put your phone in flight mode and turn off any notifications on your computer if you are using the computer for this exercise.

Answer the question as quickly as you can, allowing your inner self to answer the question. Do not analyze your thoughts but allow your intuition to flow freely. Write the answer below or in your diary.

Set a timer for 15 minutes and start writing answers to the question:

What do I want?

If you work with a partner, you can help each other do this exercise. Decide who is partner A and who is partner B. Partner B will take notes as partner A answers the question. Set a timer for 15 minutes. Partner A is going to close her (or his) eyes as partner B will ask the question "What do you want? Partner B writes as quick as she or he can and keeps asking until the timer goes off. Do not analyze, laugh, or discuss the answers yet. Just ask the question in a neutral voice. Then reverse roles for another 15 minutes with partner A asking and writing and partner B answering.

What do I want?

_____

_____

_____

_____

_____

The first time I had the vision with the eagle, I didn't act on it. But the dream kept coming back to me over and over. Eventually I got the message and knew I had to do something about it.

I had no clue about how to do it, but I knew I had always loved to support other people and help them to create a higher quality of life as an occupational therapist. Developing myself and teaching other people to live their life to the fullest was something I wanted.

I realized it was my mission to go out and develop my message to support and help other people. It aligned with what I really wanted to do, even though in that moment I could see no way how to do it. But I also knew that the "how" doesn't matter at first when your mission is strong enough, and you genuinely want the goal you set.

It is time for you to set clear, specific goals that resonate with your dreams. The next section will help you do just that.

Setting Clear, Specific Goals

In a workshop, I asked a series of questions;

- "How many of you have set a goal in the last year?"
  About ¾ of the participants raised their hands.

- "How many of you have it written down?"
  Less than half the hands stayed up.

- "How many of you had set an end date to your goal?"
  By now there were only 2 hands left. These were also the 2 participants who had achieved their goals.

How about you? How would you answer the questions above? Most people know it increases the likelihood of achieving something if we set a goal. But most people also don't know how to set a goal that is aligned with the way our brain works.

We have a very complex brain that supports our body, can make complex calculations, and makes sure we do the tasks we need to do to survive the day. But when it comes to our goals, it will only support us when we have created a clear, measurable goal that resonates with our true desire.

Without setting a goal that resonates with you, your chances of achieving anything is very low. Make sure you make your goal meaningful to you and aligned with what you want in life.

You hear many people talking about setting goals. However, the truth is that most people don't know how to set clear, specific goals that your mind can act on. Therefore, many goals are never achieved. Our mind wants to support us, but it needs clear directions.

It is easy to set goals stated like a wish – as in the wish list you just created:

- "I want to lose weight."

- "I want to stop smoking."

- "I want to run 10K."

These are not good goals. The challenge with this kind of goals is that even though you might genuinely want them, they are not *specific* enough. To achieve a goal, you need to set your inner GPS for it so you can receive clear directions. As the GPS in your car, your internal GPS is only useful if you give a clear destination.

Stating a goal using the term "I want to" does not give you a clear result. Like the rest of us, you have probably set goals that you did not achieve. How was that goal stated? Was it clear and specific, or was it stated as a "wish" goal? Let go of the goals you have set in the past and not achieved. From now on, you will know how to state your goal in the manner that helps your brain support you best.

To create an achievable goal, I recommend you set your goal as a SMART goal. Working on your goal with the procedure in this chapter makes sure your goal is clear enough to act on.

Creating a SMART Goal

SMART stands for **S**pecific, **M**easurable, **A**ctionable, **R**ealistic and **T**ime-bound.

Choose any of your wishes. As the example in this chapter, I will use a wish I often hear: The wish to lose weight. Use your own example as I break down the method to create a SMART goal.

Remember to make sure your goal is one you truly want. We discussed "should" goals in the previous chapter, and you know that these don't work.

S stands for Specific: The more specific you get, the more tangible your goal becomes. "I want to lose weight" is unclear, while "I will weigh no more than 120 pounds by December 1st, 2018" is clear.

M stands for Measurable: You need to have a very clear goal that is measurable. This means that someone could verify that you have completed or achieved it. Stating the weight you want to have reached – for example weighing no more than 120 pounds – is measurable.

It is important to note that your goal should only be measured in one dimension. Let me give an example: "I will be running 5K in 30 minutes by October 1st, 2018."

This goal is specific but measured along two dimensions: Distance and time. If you are just beginning to run, you might be capable of running 5K by October 1st. But if you do it in 35 minutes instead of the 30 minutes you stated in your goal, you will feel as though you have failed to reach your goal. Therefore, break down your overall goal into two different goals, each measured in only one dimension. Start with "I will increase my run distance to 5K by October 1st, 2018." When that is accomplished, you can set the next goal, measured by time: "I will decrease my 5K run time to under 30 minutes by February 1st, 2019." Always ask: Am I measuring my goal in only one dimension?

A stands for Actionable: Does the goal depend only on you? And can you act on it? A goal that depends on other people to do things for you or with you is not under your control. You can either set a goal together with someone else so that you are all working towards it. Or you can restate your goal so that it is under your exclusive control.

R stands for Realistic: Is this goal you have set realistic? It is not realistic to set a goal of losing 30 pounds in 30 days. However, 30 pounds in 30 weeks is an achievable goal. Establishing an appropriate time frame can make your goal realistic.

If you have poor eye vision, it is not realistic to set a goal of becoming a fighter pilot. In this case, no time frame will make the goal realistic. However, you can set a goal of finding out if eye surgery would benefit you and give you a chance of a military flying career or look for other ways of being involved with flying that you can be happy with.

T stands for time-bound: You want to have a deadline for achieving your goal. A goal without a deadline is only a wish. A deadline gets you started because you tell your brain that you do want this goal, so you better get started. You create a mental attitude that will support you.

When you set your deadline, it must be realistic and yet so close that it gives you a push to move forward. In the weight-loss example, losing one pound a week is reasonable. If you know it is going to be an ongoing diet for many weeks, break it down to smaller goals that you can accomplish and create a win situation. Remember it is hard to lose weight over holidays and adjust your time accordingly.

A test you can do for yourself to determent if your goal is SMART is this: Imagine I am meeting you after the goal is supposed to be completed. I know your goal. When I ask you if you have achieved it, can you answer with a clear yes or no?

A great goal is a goal that is far enough outside of your comfort zone to force you to stretch, but still within your reach.

Setting Goals About Personal Growth

Setting a goal around personal growth can be a challenge. The key here is to realize what it means for you to grow personally. What can you accomplish when you have expanded your comfort zone?

If one of your wishes is to have more self-esteem, you must look at what high self-esteem is for you. For instance, is it essential to be able to speak in public? If so, you might want to set a goal around speaking in public. Is it to prove to yourself you can take on a physical challenge? Then your goal might be to set a goal in that area.

Look back at your dream exercise and use the way you saw yourself being changed as a guide for setting your goals. If you feel your goal is big, don't worry. I will show you how you can break such a goal into smaller goals in just a few pages.

Here are some examples of personal goals you can use directly or tweak to fit your situation. When you fill in a date for these goals, choose one far enough out to make the goal realistic yet close enough to make you start working on your goal.

- ✔ By <Insert date> I will have spoken to at least one person I don't know.

- ✔ By <insert date> I will have called an old friend I haven't spoken with for years.

- ✔ By <insert date> I will do something <insert what you specifically want> that makes me feel good.

- ✔ By <insert date> I will have done the mirror exercise (as described in chapter 4) 30 days in a row.

✔ By <insert date> I will have signed up for an in-person class on (choose something of interest for you – exercise class, arts and craft, cooking, etc.)

Other goals to grow yourself personally can focus on any kind of physical challenge, from taking a 15-minute walk to running a marathon. You might be standing up for yourself at work, speaking up at a meeting, calling someone, going somewhere, or doing something that you have been putting off for a long time.

Exercise 16: Setting a Clear and Measurable Goal

Now it's your turn. Take one of your items from your wish list that you want to achieve.

Write your goal here and make sure it is **S**pecific, **M**easurable, **A**ctionable, **R**ealistic and **T**ime-bound:

My goal:

_____

_____

or something even better.

Make sure that your goal is SMART by answering the following questions:

My goal is

✔ Specific because _____

✔ Measurable because _____

✔ Actionable because _____

- ✔ Realistic because _____

- ✔ Time-bound because _____

Example from one of my goals: By June 20th, 2015 at 6am I will have accomplished a 50K run or something better.

This goal is

- ✔ **Specific** because it states that I will have accomplished a specific task, in this case, a specific race that took place through the night of June 19th.

- ✔ **Measurable** because it states what I will do and when.

- ✔ **Actionable** because there is a specific event to work towards, making it easy to plan my training towards achieving the goal.

- ✔ **Realistic** because I set this goal in September of 2014 and was in basic running shape.

- ✔ **Time-bound** because there is a specific date and time when I will have accomplished it.

A perfect goal is one that forces you to stretch outside your comfort zone but still feels doable, even if right now you don't know exactly how. If your goal feels too big, you will want to break it down into more achievable goals and actions as I will show you in the next section.

Lotte's Tip

You might have noted that I often write "or something better" after I have stated my goals. This leaves the possibility for you to achieve your goal faster and/or easier than you have imagined. As you have written your goal, so it feels right, complete it with the words "or something better."

Breaking Your Goals into More Tangible Goals

Goals come in many sizes. Sometimes they are bigger than you can manage right away. I have a goal of having spoken in front of 20,000 people by December 31st, 2020 or something even better. Goals like this are so large they might stop you in your tracks before you even get started.

I decided to break this long-term goal into smaller goals which are somewhat more actionable and seemed more achievable for me.

Having big goals can be challenging and motivating at the same time. Breaking your goals into easy-to-reach tangible goals is a great way to support you moving forward.

In my example goal of speaking, I have had several goals over the past 5 years. Most of these goals have been used to push myself out of my comfort zone and to train my voice. I have been using the tools you will learn in part 3 of this book to work on my internal fear of speaking and to grow my self-worth and self-esteem.

Some of my goals have been:

- By December 12th, 2012, I will have completed a speaker training

- By December 12th, 2013, I will have given 5 public speeches or something better

- In 2017 my goal was: By December 12th, 2017 I will have given 20 public speeches or something better

Every year, I am setting a least one new and increased goal of speaking to keep pushing my comfort zone and grow. And every year, I find myself being better and more at ease with public speaking. I know I am on the right track to achieving my goal. In the beginning, the groups were small. Today I have spoken to grade

6, high school kids, and seniors, in front of groups from 10 people to more than 200 at a time.

Writing this book, I broke my overall goal down into smaller goals like, "I will have completed my first draft by February 16th, 2018." This made the writing more achievable for me. This helped me know that I was moving towards my overall goal: "By December 31st, 2018 my book *Life after Bullying* will be published or something better." It also kept me moving forward instead of procrastinating when the writing didn't flow the way I wanted.

Action Steps

Another way to break down your goals into something more tangible is to create action steps. In this case, you keep your overall goal in mind but focus on the next specific action.

An action step around writing my book sounded like this:

- "For the next two weeks, I will write for a minimum of 30 minutes every day." Note that I don't push it too far. The purpose is to take this action step then decide on the next step. The next step might be similar, or it could be different as I learned from my previous experience.

An action step doesn't have to relate to a specific goal. It can stand alone when needed. For example, an action step around a wish to increase self-esteem around other people could be:

- "At the next <event> by <date>, I will speak to one person I didn't know beforehand, or something even better." Note that I don't state for how long I will speak, as this isn't under my control. This action step forces me to go up and speak to someone, even if it is only for a brief minute.

Congratulations on having set at least one goal. You can choose to keep it this way or set more goals. There are different schools of thought about how many goals one should set. I say that less is more: do not set more than five overall goals at a time and having one goal is just fine. Choose your action steps accordingly. Even if you have more than one goal you want to achieve, focusing on one of them at a time is the best way to move forward.

When you look at your wish list, you might find you can create many goals from it. This is fine. Prioritize which one to five goals are the most important right now. Then keep the list for future use and go back to it whenever you have achieved a goal.

Carry a list with your current goal with you in your purse or pocket and look at it every morning and every evening before you go to bed. Visualize you have achieved your goal as described in the next chapter.

Summary

You have discovered what you genuinely want to achieve. You have created a list of your deepest wishes and learned the power of setting clear and measurable goals.

By now, you should have at least one goal written down and stated as a SMART goal. Keep this goal in mind as you continue to learn about tools that will support you in achieving your goals.

A great goal is one that supports you in moving forward and pushes you outside your comfort zone so that you can change and grow.

Lotte's Strategies to Increase Your Quality of Life

- ✔ Take time to research your true desires.

- ✔ Allow yourself to dream – even big dreams.

- ✔ Give yourself permission to paint your future as you would love to create it.

- ✔ Be willing to take small steps outside your comfort zone to achieve your dreams.

- ✔ Aligning your goals with what is truly meaningful to you increases your chance of achieving your goal and makes life more fun and easy.

- ✔ Create specific and clear goals by using the SMART model.

Chapter 7

Achieving Your Goal

"What you get by achieving your goals is not as important as what you become by achieving your goals."

ZIG ZIGLAR

Using Action Steps to Achieve Your Goal

I shook with fear as I gave my first speech. My palms where sweaty. What was I doing believing that I could stand up and speak in front of even a small crowd of 12 people like this? As I spoke, I gained more confidence. I realized my audience was listening to what I had to say. As I left the meeting that evening, I felt high. The adrenaline was still rushing through my body, and I couldn't stop smiling. Several people had shared what they took away from my speech to start using in their life. And I realized I loved supporting people by sharing my story and tangible action steps.

That evening, I accomplished my first big goal in public speaking. For some, that might not sound amazing, but for me, it was a step far outside my comfort zone. Before I stood up in front of even this little crowd of people, I had gone through several stages. I had broken my goal down into manageable action steps.

Every goal has a list of action steps to it. It might be creating a diet plan if you want to lose weight, or an exercise plan when you want to start exercising. In this case, I had to conquer my voice, work on my social anxiety, reach out to find a place to speak, and finally deliver a speech. All were sub-goals necessary to be able to achieve my "big" goal.

Feeling Scared About Your Goal?

In the last chapter, you created a least one goal. I invite you to go back and look at your goal: When you read it – how do you feel inside? A great goal is a goal that makes you feel a little scared. Can I really achieve this? This is because a great goal is a goal that pushes you outside your comfort zone. If it is easy to reach, it will not be changing your life in the way you truly want.

I have often heard people with low self-esteem say things like: "It can't be a goal worth accomplishing just to sign up and be part a class for four hours." You should not beat yourself up like that. This is a great goal. When you have social anxiety as I had, just signing up for a class is a huge accomplishment. Congratulate yourself and keep moving.

A great goal – a goal that is worth achieving – is a goal that makes you tingle inside, feeling a little scared and unsure if you can make it. Your comfort zone is telling you to stay safe, but when you want to move forward and live a life worth living, you must move just a little outside of your comfort zone. This is what personal growth is about.

When I started my journey, I had small goals like, "Speak up once at our next meeting," or, "approach another mother at the playground." These were scary goals for me at that time.

Conquering Your Goal

I had a goal of public speaking. When I finally realized I had a message and sharing it with the world would help people to grow their self-esteem, I was terrified. I wrote this massive goal of speaking to 20,000 people and pushed the date out in the future. As I had only spoken publicly once at the time I wrote this goal, it was way outside my comfort zone. I broke the goal down into smaller, more manageable goals that pushed me forward towards the larger overall goal.

You can always take your goal and chunk it down into more achievable goals.

One of my smaller goals was to speak to 5 groups during one year. Even this goal felt like an enormous challenge. I was still dealing with anxiety and still did not believe much in myself. Over the preceding years, I had worked on my anxiety and my voice. It had become better, but to speak in public was something else entirely and to call someone asking for a speaking engagement was scary.

Taking my goal and breaking it down into manageable action steps meant going through the following questions and answering them as honestly as I could.

What obstacles exist that I need to address?

- I feel I'm not a good speaker

- I don't trust in my own ability

What can I do to address these obstacles?

- Take speaking training

- Find ways to raise my internal trust

What actions steps do I have to do to achieve my goals?

- Research speaking training by March 1st

- Sign up for a speaking training by April 1st

- Research tools that could help me raise my self-esteem by February 1st

- Start doing exercises to increase my self-esteem by February 2nd

- Create the topic for a speech by April 20th

- Look for places to speak for free by May 1st

- Call one or more potential places to speak by May 5st

To feel a sense of success, I started with calling just one place by May 5th. Note that I wrote "or more" to open up the possibility of calling more places. As the first action step – to call – was achieved, I set a new one. This time, my action step was to call three or more places by May 15th. My end goal was to have called at least 20 places by the end of June to line up speaking appointment in the fall.

The following form helps you create an action plan like mine. When you fill out the form, be as thorough as you can. You can achieve your goal much easier when you know *exactly* the steps to take and have set internal deadlines.

As you fill it out, you might feel fear rising up to make you want to either drop your goal or push your deadlines far into the future. These fears are caused by your limiting beliefs about your own ability.

I will take you through several techniques that you can use to work on this fear, methods that have been really helpful for both myself and my clients. For now, you can choose to go back to Chapter Three, to the exercise "Notice How You Feel" and use the technique of breathing through your fear to let go just for now.

Exercise 17: Action Plan

My goal: _____

What obstacles do I need to address to achieve my goal?

Obstacle #1: _____

Obstacle #2: _____

Obstacle #3: _____

What can I do to address these obstacles? By when will I do it?

#1 _____ By: _____

#2 _____ By: _____

#3 _____ By: _____

What action steps will I have to do to achieve my goal? By when will I do them?

Action step: _____ By: _____

Action step: _____ By: _____

Action step: _____ By: _____

Action step: _____ By: _____

Action step: _____ By: _____

The more you write on your action plan, the easier it becomes to reach your goal. Write down whatever comes to you, no matter if it is a seemingly small thing. When you get the inspiration or insight then it is something to be aware of. In Denmark the weather can sometimes be an obstacle to getting out. By being aware, the simple solution is to buy proper gear.

> **Lotte's Tip**
>
> The more detailed you can get when creating your plan, the easier it will be to achieve your goal. It doesn't matter if you can't think of all the steps you need to take to accomplish your goal right now. Make a note in your calendar two weeks in the future and see if there is something more you want to add now that you have had this goal in mind for a little while.

Minimum/Target/Outrageous Goals

One way to work with limiting beliefs is to divide your goals into a minimum, a target, and an outrageous goal.

One of my latest goals was to challenge myself and see if I could complete a 50-kilometer ultramarathon. I set a goal, "On June 22th at 5.30 am, I will have run the 50K coast to coast challenge."

This was a goal I had a hard time believing I could achieve, and this belief was holding me back. When I reframed it into a minimum goal (accomplish it in whatever time it would take), a target (running it in 7 hours) and outrageous (running it in 6 hours or less, being able to stand on the finishing line watching the sunrise over the ocean), it seemed more doable. I would envision myself completing the outrageous goal but would be content with the minimum goal.

Not every goal is amenable to this kind of goal setting. Sometimes it is better to state a goal ending with the term, "or something even better." In the case of my goal to complete five speaking engagements, I stated my goal as, "by December 12th, 2013, I will have completed five public speeches or something better." This meant opening my mind to getting more speaking engagements than the five I was aiming for.

Settings minimum/target/outrageous goals has worked well for my goal of starting to speak with people; A minimum goal for approaching people at the playground for me was to make eye contact and smile. The target goal was to approach one person and say at least one sentence. The outrageous goal was to engage in a more extended conversation.

If you find it difficult to begin working on one of your goals, this can be a great way to get started. Think of the absolute minimum work you can do to move forward and state this as your minimum goal. Your target is what you would prefer to have done, and the outrageous is equal to what will make you feel you have achieved something utterly extraordinary.

Do you have a goal you can break into three: Minimum, Target, Outrageous? Choose one goal you want to accomplish and write down your three goals.

Exercise 18: Minimum/Target/Outrageous Goals

My goal: _____

My **minimum** goal: _____

My **target** goal: _____

My **outrageous** goal: _____

Dividing your goal into the three different possibilities works well with creating action steps. For example, if you want to start running and it is a challenge just getting out of the door, your minimum action step can be changing into your running gear. As you don your gear, you are more likely to go for a short run, or even just a walk.

Lotte's Tip

The principle of Minimum/Target/Outrageous works great for projects too. You might have a report due in a few weeks. Here you can set a daily **minimum** goal to work on it for 10 minutes, your **target** goal might be to work on it for half an hour, and your **outrageous** could be to spend two hours on the project.

Envisioning Your Goal As Complete

"I'm standing in an auditorium in front of 400 people. I am sharing stories, tips, and insights on how to move through your past and live a fulfilling life. The people in front of me are engaged, taking part in the exercises and taking notes. I feel empowered, happy, and honored to be able to support people in their internal growth."

This is the vision that inspires and moves me forward towards my goal of speaking to 20,000 people. Over the years, I have gone from social anxiety to having a passion for speaking and teaching. My vision inspires me to act and continually move outside my comfort zone, creating win after win.

Creating a vision of what it looks like when you have achieved your goal is a great supportive tool. My vision of speaking to 400 people came to me in my dream meditation several times and is very vivid to me. Even though I have not spoken to 400 people at the same time yet, I have spoken to 140 high school students at one time and all 400 high school students at this level over 2 days. I feel well on my way to one day standing on a stage in front of 400 or more people.

You might have a vision equally inspiring to you from the dream exercise earlier. Otherwise, I invite you to create one through the vision exercise that follows in a few pages.

Your Vision Becomes Your GPS

Envisioning your goal as complete supports your inner GPS because you now have an internal vision of where you want to go. Several pieces of research have shown that our brain can't tell the difference between a mental image and reality. The more complete and detailed you can create the vision, the more support you get from your unconscious mind.

As you program your inner self by envisioning your goal as complete, you start getting ideas about how you can accomplish the goal. You might also have a little voice coming up telling you to shut up, "There is no way you can do this, so why do you even try?" For now, you can work with this voice of doubt by simply stating, "This is ok, I hear you – but for now I choose to believe I can achieve my goal."

Lotte's Tip

Feel the feelings you will feel once you have achieved your goal. Will you be proud? Happy? Grateful? Joyful? Honored to be able to experience the moment? Valuable? Find the triggers that really make you feel and own that you have achieved your goal.

This is one of the cornerstones to envisioning and fulfilling your goals. When we truly see, believe, and feel ourselves having achieved our goal, our mind can't differentiate this from reality. It will do its best to support us fulfilling this vision, opening our minds for inspiration and possible action steps towards our dream.

Wearing Your New Dress at the Special Event

When you envision your goal as complete, adding a particular feeling is a wonderful way to enhance this vision. Let's say your goal is to lose 30 pounds. Now envision yourself at your new weight, how you feel proud and confident. Envision yourself going into your favorite store, buying a dress that fits your new size, imagine what it looks like when you try it on, notice how it looks on your new body and how it feels on your skin. Envision later wearing this dress at a special event. You feel confident in your new size and are proud of your accomplishment when you look in your mirror.

Another example of this could be if you suffer from social anxiety and don't take your kids to amusement parks, because it is too uncomfortable for you. Visualize and feel how your kids' faces shine as they go through the park hand in hand with you and how you feel at ease and happy. Keep the images with you as you work towards your goal.

My vision for speaking to other mothers at the playground went like this: Each morning I would envision myself being at our favorite playground watching the kids playing. I would then imagine seeing another mother standing alone, walking over to her and starting to speak. Asking questions like, "How old is your daughter?" and imagining how I would feel confident and at peace talking with her. This vision gave me the courage to speak to another mother in real life too.

Now it is your turn to create your vision. You want to make it as big and bright as you can to turn on your inner GPS. It can never be too bright. Know you can always come back and expand it as you grow.

Exercise 19: Envisioning Your Goal Achieved

Start by reading through the whole exercise.

Visualize that you have achieved your goal. See yourself acting and doing the things you will be doing at that time. Notice what it looks like and feels like having accomplished your goal. Close your eyes for a few minutes, if you are in a place where it is safe to do so, and see with your inner eyes what accomplishing your goal looks like. Sense the feelings attached to this accomplishment.

Now complete the following sentences as best as you can right now. Add as many descriptive words as possible.

My goal is: _____

The way it will look when I have achieved this goal is:

_____

_____

The way I will feel when I have achieved this goal is:

_____

_____

My vision: _____

_____

_____

_____

_____

> Well done. Now use this vision by spending a few minutes every morning and evening to see and feel your goal achieved.

Creating Reminders to Inspire Your Daily Actions

Visuals

"As I look at the soaring eagle, I am reminded of my vision. I close my eyes and allow myself to become the speaker on the stage. I feel the feelings and experience the applause."

Using visuals is a great way to remind yourself of your vision. This visual can be an object or an image that symbolizes your goal. For me, a soaring eagle symbolizes my goal of speaking because this powerful bird showed up several times when I went through the dream exercises. When you think back at the dream exercise in Chapter Six, what image comes to mind that represent your goal?

You can easily go online and find free pictures you can use as a screensaver or print out. I've used www.pixabay.com for many of the images I use to support my goals, and there are many similar sources of free images on the internet. Search for a topic and find a photo that resonates with you.

Affirmations

Affirmations are another way to keep yourself on track. An affirmation is a compelling sentence that anchors your goal as if you have already achieved it. For example, I anchor my vision above by saying my affirmation out load: "I am so happy and grateful that I now am able to empower others and speak confidently in front of thousands of people around the world."

It is important to state your affirmations as if you have already achieved your goal. An easy and yet powerful way to create your affirmations is to start with the words, "I am so happy and grateful that I now..." Then write your affirmation in positive terms and include one or more words that describe your feelings.

Some of my affirmations over the years have been:

- ✔ I am so happy and grateful that I now feel relaxed and confident as I speak in front of an audience.

- ✔ I am so happy and grateful that I now enjoy the sunrise after having completed the 50-kilometer ultramarathon.

- ✔ I am so happy and grateful that I now feel relaxed as I speak to other mothers at the playground.

Exercise 20: Create Your Own Affirmation

Now it is your turn to create an affirmation. Take your goal and answer the following questions:

What is the result of having achieved your goal?

_____

How do you want to feel when you have achieved your goal?

_____

Now write down your affirmation by completing the sentence below:

I am so happy and grateful that I now

_____

_____

Images and affirmations help you remember your goals and visions. You can use a three by five index card to write down your affirmation and include the picture you have chosen. Create one card for each goal if you have more than one. Before you go to sleep, flip through your cards and envision yourself having achieved your goals.

You can also use your photos to create a collage with pictures, key words or affirmations. This is sometimes called a *vision board*. If you create one, place it where you see it daily. The collage can contain several pictures representing the same goal. In my case, it has images of the soaring eagle, myself on a stage, and a picture of an audience all representing the same goal. You can create a new vision board as often as you like. I take a picture of mine and use this as the background photo on my computer and tablet. This is a great way to ensure that you are constantly reminded of your vision.

Lotte's Tip

Copy your affirmations onto sticky notes and place them around the house. It can be on the bathroom mirror, in your wardrobe or closet. Put them in places you often see to be reminded of your goal. I have affirmations and affirming pictures that come up as my screensaver. You can also have a picture in a frame beside your workspace to remind you of one of your goals or use an electronic picture frame that rotates all your goal pictures.

The Path to Achieve Your Goal

One day, my husband told me about this particular race called coast-to-coast. This was a 50-kilometer race – an ultramarathon. You started at sunset on the west coast of Denmark, watching the sun set in the sea, and ran eastwards through the summer night to face the rising sun the next morning on the opposite coast. This race was not about winning – they didn't even time it – it was all about the experience.

I had never run a race before, and it wasn't even on my radar to do so. But for some reason, I was intrigued and started to practice. When I started, I could run 5 kilometers without stopping, then I went up to 6 kilometers, and soon I could even do 9 kilometers with some alternation between running and walking at the end.

Then I came to a point when I kept making excuses for myself. I had excellent excuses: A typical Danish winter is cold, rainy, windy, and dark. And I kept holding myself back. Then I realized that I didn't honestly believe I could do it. I was stuck, and my subconscious mind was holding me back.

I decided to take a more in-depth look at what was holding me back. I looked at my goal, and it was stated in all the right terms. However, my inner self, when I listened to that little voice as I said my goal out loud, told me: "There is no way you can do this, this is an ultramarathon for ultra-tough runners, and you have never even run a race before." So, along with my running training, I started working on my inner beliefs. Over the next couple of weeks, I managed to change and began to believe that I could really do it.

First, I created a minimum, target, and outrageous goal. That helped as I was pretty sure that I at least could walk the 50 kilometers.

Next, I did the same things that I did in my recovering process to raise my inner beliefs. This is the same thing as I will be teaching you in the next chapters.

- I started to focus on my words: What was I telling myself consciously and subconsciously.

- I used tapping (which you learn about in Chapter Ten). Using the tapping technique, I worked with the limiting statements: "I am not able to run 50 kilometers," "Who do you think you are, believing you can run all through the night," and, "It feels awful having to train in the cold rainy weather."

- I used my own releasing process, which you learn about in Chapter Twelve.

- I visualized the ideal outcome, including the feelings and sounds, as you just learned above.

Slowly at first and then more quickly I started to change. I got outside running, and I began to enjoy it. I created a training program and kept working on the inner as well as the outer condition.

Never Beat Yourself Up

We set goals and sometimes we don't achieve them. Things outside of our control can happen, or we believed we could achieve it in a specific timeframe and it proved to take longer. Too often we beat ourselves up for not meeting our goals. Instead, we should evaluate and restate our goals.

One way to work around this is to have a *high intention* but *low attachment*. For example, I had a high intention of completing this ultramarathon. I had worked hard to achieve my goal, and I wanted to be able to stand on the finishing line knowing that I had proven to myself that I could do this.

Yet, things can go wrong. What if I had sprained my ankle or tripped and hurt myself, being unable to complete the race? If I were too fixated on my goal, it would be easy for me to consider myself a failure. This is where having low attachment to your goal comes in. If you don't achieve your goal on time, having low attachment allows you to review it and see what needs to change without blaming yourself.

Maybe you want to do some more inner work. Perhaps you are doing all the right things, but it just takes a little longer than you thought, and you are well on your way. Focus on what you have achieved on your way to reaching your goal. Then either leave the goal because it is no longer essential or restate it with a new deadline.

Taking Up the Challenge

Race day came, and I was ready, or so I thought. I hadn't anticipated how hard it would be to start running a 50K race at a time when I would usually be in my bed sleeping. Sunset was at 10.22pm. In the gorgeous sunset, I was part of a pack of more than 3,000 runners who hit the road. It was an unforgettable experience. The running went fine for the first 25 kilometers. Then fatigue set in. At the 30-kilometer mark, I started to walk and must admit I walked most of the last 20 kilometers.

I did complete all 50 kilometers of the ultramarathon. Even though it was not precisely in the way I had envisioned, I was thrilled. I had managed to push myself through this physical experience, growing both personally and physically. My minimum goal was to complete the run, and I did that. And I learned a lot about myself and my abilities in the process.

It was a beautiful night and one that will stick with me forever. The sunset was beautiful, and all through the night, the sky was light to the north, giving us light enough to stay on the path without even using our flashlights. Listening to the birds going to bed, and later their wakeup sounds was a fantastic experience. Apart from the birds, everything else was quiet in the countryside, something you usually never experience.

Even if I hadn't accomplished my 50K goal, I would still have grown a lot. In the process, I had become healthier and stronger. I had more energy as I was moving outside of my comfort zone and pushing my limits even further for each month. This growth is the ultimate goal. Will I pass the finish line? In this case, I did. But even if I hadn't, no one could take away the growth I had experienced in my process, and that is really the most important part of any goal.

Now it is your turn to start completing your goals. As we move into Part Three, you will learn several tools you can use to push through your obstacles and grow yourself in the process.

Look at your goal or goals. And choose one goal you want to start with. Many people find it hard to work on multiple goals at one time, and the more goals you work on, the higher the risk that you won't be working on any of them.

As you look at your goal and action plan, think about the next action step you need to take and keep this in mind as you read Part Three.

Summary

You have learned about creating action steps, about being open to any obstacles that might get in your way, and how to plan for them. You have learned about breaking a goal into a minimum goal, a target goal, and an outrageous goal to support your move forward.

You have planned to achieve your goal and created a vision of what it feels like when you have accomplished it.

Throughout Part Two, you have created a blueprint for your success. By now you know what gives your life meaning and have created one or more goals and the action steps to achieve your goals.

Together, Parts One and Two have helped you establish a strong foundation and to know your desired outcome. Now it is your turn to achieve your goals and create the life you truly deserve.

Part Three will give you a list of tools you can use to support you in moving forward and increase your trust in your own ability to grow.

Lotte's Strategies to Increase Your Quality of Life

- ✔ Create a vision of what you truly desire.

- ✔ See your vision every night before you fall asleep.

- ✔ Allow yourself to feel the emotions you will experience when you achieve your goal as you see your vision.

- ✔ Find pictures or items that remind you of your vision. Place them around your house and carry them with you on 3 x 5 index cards.

- ✔ Create an action plan.

- ✔ Create affirmations and read these daily. You can also place these around your home by copying them onto sticky notes.

- ✔ Congratulate yourself on each little step you take towards your goal – and on every win, big or small.

Part Three

Building Your Ideal Life

Chapter 8

Build Your New Life

"Life is like riding a bicycle. To keep your balance, you must keep moving."

ALBERT EINSTEIN

Introduction to Part Three

For many years, I didn't realize how much impact having been bullied had on me, and how it affected my internal and external reaction to life. My hushed voice, social anxiety and bodily responses to things that were going on around me could have given me a clue if I had thought about it. But I believed that was just how I was created.

When I first started my work to grow personally, I started with working on the symptoms. My sleeping disorder, anxiety, and low self-esteem were noticeable and gave me tangible clues what to work on. In this part of *Life After Bullying*, you will learn several tools to work on the things you are aware of. These tools can support you to grow your life.

Often, we know our symptoms and work on these, even though we don't quite realize why we have them in the first place. I didn't know being bullied was the root of all my problems. What I know today is that being bullied is a traumatic event. It leaves a mark on you that can stay with you until you do something about it and work through it.

When you're in a situation with high emotions, where you don't feel safe, and can't see how you can escape, you perceive this as traumatic. When you are bullied, it might not seem like a big event in that moment, depending on the severity of the bullying. But most often, bullying happens at school, in regularly occurring activities, at work, or even at home. This means that you must go back to this place over and over, exposing yourself to the situation again and again. These seemingly small situations add up and eventually leave a major impact on you.

When I was bullied, it created a lot of emotions I did my best not to show. I did not feel safe in my classroom anymore. There was no escape because I had to go back to my class and that teacher day after day. Every day was a repetition of the day before, causing me to really embed that traumatic memory on a deep level. A lot of blockages were created in my body, leaving an impact on me for many years.

When the emotions get stuck in the body, they are likely to get in the way whenever you want to change. As you work through these exercises, be aware of your emotions. Allow yourself to feel them and work through these as you move forward.

Your Toolbox for Success

This part of the book is a bit different from the previous two parts. I am giving you a toolbox with various tools to use to reach your goal. Some of these tools are quite expansive, like tapping and RIM. Others are simpler. In each chapter, you will be introduced to techniques you can use right away. On the book website, you will find a list of references if you want to learn more.

You can choose to work your way through each chapter, learning and using the tools one by one as you go through the remainder of this book. Or you can read through every chapter once and then pick the tools that appeal most to you and start there.

If you feel that one tool is not for you, just skip past it for now. Come back when you have experienced some personal growth and try it out again. I have often been introduced to techniques I was not ready for, but which later became useful and quite powerful. Play around with the tools, be open-minded, and listen to your intuition as you experiment with the different tools.

As you grow, your toolbox will expand. Even if there is just one tool you feel works for you today, use this tool as much as possible for the next month or two. Then come back and look for the next step to take.

In Honor of Your Progress

Congratulations on coming this far, you are indeed moving forward in your life. Remember to keep track of every little step forward you take so you can look back for inspiration when you feel stuck. Always keep in mind that personal growth is a stepwise process. It can seem slow, especially if you work on your own, but the changes are accumulating and will be long-lasting.

Feel free to send me an email at lotte@lifeafterbullying.com with your personal experience and success stories.

In the past chapters, I walked you through some tools I hope you have started using. I gave you these tools immediately, so you could experience personal growth right away. For your convenience, I made a list of the tools from the previous chapters below, together with the chapter they appear in. If you haven't yet started using these tools, I recommend you go back and pick at least one tool to start implementing today.

Tools from the Previous Chapters

Chapter One

- ✔ Journaling (page 12)

Chapter Two

- ✔ Finding Yourself (page 20)
- ✔ Changing Your Reactions (page 28)
- ✔ Preparing for Success (page 33)

Chapter Three

- ✔ Uncover Your Limiting Beliefs (page 41)
- ✔ Acknowledge Your Current Situation (page 44)
- ✔ Notice How You Feel (page 49)
- ✔ Discovering Your Uniqueness (page 52)

Chapter Four

- ✔ Placing Your Voice (page 64)
- ✔ Mirror Exercise (page 69)

Chapter Five

- ✔ Find Meaning in Your Life (page 85)

Chapter Six

- ✔ Dream Exercise (page 94)
- ✔ Create A List of Your Deepest Wishes (page 96)
- ✔ Setting A Clear and Measurable Goal (page 103)

Chapter Seven

- ✔ Action Plan (page 113)
- ✔ Minimum/Target/Outrageous Goals (page 115)
- ✔ Envision Your Goal Achieved (page 119)
- ✔ Create Your Own Affirmation (page 121)

Chapter 9

Creating Time for You

"Hope has two beautiful daughters. Their names are anger and courage; anger at the way things are, and courage to see that they do not remain the way they are."

St. Augustine

"My mom said I could only invite 12, so you can't come," said Kirsten, pointing at me. Once again, I was left out. Putting on a fake smile, I walked away. Having been rejected so often, you would think I was getting used to it. But no. As I walked away, my soul hurt, and I was fighting back the tears.

Have you ever experienced being left out when everybody else was invited to a party? Selected last or not at all for a team? Or had a group be forced to take you in, making group activities painful?

Being rejected is painful – very painful. It leaves scars and a deep longing to belong. After a while, you reach a point where you want to belong no matter what. This often leads you to develop what I call "the pleaser syndrome." We start to say "Yes" to every opportunity to support others, afraid of the consequence if we say "No."

You often end up in the outer circle. You don't really belong, and you do things you don't want to do. The result can be a loss of integrity, trying even harder to please, and increased body stress.

Trying always to be nice, to always offer my assistance, didn't really help, but it was the only way I knew. Growing up, I continued this pattern of sacrificing my own life.

How about you? Have you developed pleaser syndrome? Do you always strive to belong? Do you say "Yes" to people when you want to say "No"? Are you losing your own integrity because you want to belong no matter the cost?

When Pleasing Becomes Your Lifestyle

I was guiding a group through an exercise when I noticed one of the participants getting a more and more puzzled facial expression. Afterward, she shared the profound insight she had received:

"I have always been the one that helped out. In every family gathering, I am expected to do most of the work. My grandmother relies on me to take her everywhere even though I have a job, and my friends always take advantage of me. I always wanted to please and thought that it was my calling to be of service to others. And now I realize that it isn't and that I have been lying to myself to please others. I now realize what this has cost me in lack of integrity for myself, lack of energy, and increased stress. There always seems to be something I should do for others, and I have never time to do what I love."

Can you relate to this? Getting to the point where you realize you are cheating yourself can be tough. Remember, up until now you have done what you thought was best for you. From now on, you can look forward and improve your life one step at a time. Your journey to living the life you deserve has started, and you are making progress with every step. Go easy on yourself and celebrate every little win.

Get to Know How You Spend Your Time

It's easy to end up living your life on autopilot. You do many things out of habit, often not even aware of why you spend your time the way you do. Of course, your work takes away a certain number of hours a week, and your role as a mother, father, wife or husband might take another bite of the week. But how do you spend the rest?

The following exercise is designed to help you realize how you are spending your time. It is essential to really be true to yourself about this. The purpose is to free up time for you to do what you value the most.

Exercise 21: How Do I Spend My Day?

Write down how you spend your time on a daily, weekly, and monthly basis

How many hours overtime hours do you put in per week? _____

How many hours do you spend volunteering? _____

How many hours do you spend supporting family members and friends outside your own home? _____

What other things comes to your mind that you spend time on?

_____

Now answer the following questions:

How does this use of time make you feel?

_____

What does this use of time cost you in money, stress, or time away from your family?

_____

Can any of these tasks be done by someone else?

_____

What can you do today to free up one hour a week you can use for your own purposes?

_____

I am in favor of volunteering and supporting friends and family. But you need to spend your time wisely. You should do things you love and that match your specific skills. You also need to be aware how many hours a week/month you have available to spend if there is to be any time left over for yourself.

You might end up saying "No" to much of what you are doing today and look for something completely different. Ideally, you want to do things where you know you can make a difference to someone doing something you really love to do, using your unique skills.

Take Back Your Time

Taking your life back and creating time for yourself is the route to living a more fulfilling life. When you know what is important to you, you will have more energy, create quality time and be able to stay in tune with yourself and your family.

Taking back your time is a vital part of healing yourself. When you keep doing things only to please other people, how can you truly love yourself? You don't stay true to yourself. You don't honor yourself for what you are worth. On an unconscious level, you are telling yourself you are not worthy of living the life you desire.

You are worthy of living a fulfilling life. You deserve to have the best. Taking back your time is a process. You slowly start saying "No" and then create the life you want to live. You need to know what a fulfilling life means for you. Not what it is like for your friends, or your partner, or for some celebrity, but for you. The way you like to spend your time is most likely different from how I want to spend my time. Knowing how to live a fulfilling life gives you a yardstick to guide you when people ask for your help.

Exercise 22: My Daily Life

Set aside half an hour of undisturbed time to do this exercise. Put your phone in flight mode and turn off any notifications. Put on some relaxing music and make yourself comfortable.

Start by reading through the entire exercise. Now go through each question one by one. Read it, close your eyes and sense the answer. Write down whatever comes to your mind as fully as possible.

I wake up in the morning and realize my day is going to be a great day. The first thing I do is

_____

As I move into the day, I am focused and alert. When I get home from work, I spend the rest of the day doing

_____ and _____

During my week, I prioritize spending time with

_____

During my week, I prioritize doing these things for myself that uplift me and give me energy

_____

I have these ideas and this inspiration to create a life for myself that is fulfilling and uplifting

_____

Great work.

Make Your Life Important to You – Learn to Say "No"

Many people find it hard to say "No." It is especially difficult when we have a yearning to belong no matter what. Saying "Yes" feels easier in the moment. However, the cost of your commitment shows up later when you must do the tasks you agreed to. Learning to say "No" will support you in freeing up your time to work on your own personal development. It will also free up time to do what you love to do. In the beginning, it often requires a good deal of courage to say "No." Luckily, there are some techniques you can use to make it easier.

When you have suffered from pleaser syndrome for a while, saying "No" is likely to bring up some negative emotions. It is a good idea to have an answer prepared. A very usable reply whenever someone asks if you can do something, say

"I am not sure I have the time.
Let me think about it and get back to you with my answer."

You have not turned the request down and have bought yourself time to think about whether you honestly want to do it or not.

Decision Support Techniques

- Make yourself a priority list. One of my priorities is to give back to the community in places where my kids are involved.

- Ask yourself if the task is aligned with your core values and based on your heart's desire.

- Make a list of "don't do." It can be helpful to make a list of the things that you don't like or want to do, but that you might previously have agreed to. In the future, make a promise to yourself to say "No" to anything on that list.

- Know how many hours on a weekly or monthly basis you want to use serving others. Do not go beyond this amount of time.

- When in doubt, say "No." You can always come back later with a yes – it is harder to turn a yes into a no.

When you have made your decision following your decision support list, call back or send a message with your reply. A definite no (or yes) will in most cases be enough. Do not make excuses. If pressed, appreciate the value of what the other person is asking, but repeat that you must decline. "Collecting money for the soccer club trip is a really valuable task. Unfortunately, I am not able to help."

> **Lotte's Tip**
>
> Whenever you feel the urge to say "Yes" ask the following questions to make sure you are doing so for the right reasons. And that you are not agreeing out of habit or due to "pleaser syndrome."
>
> - Am I afraid of what will happen if I say "No"?
>
> - Does saying "Yes" serve my family, my values, or my own life and personal development?

Remember to congratulate yourself for taking this huge step in creating time for yourself. Learning to say "No" is a process. Congratulate yourself every time you decide based on your own goals and desires. The more you practice, the easier it becomes.

As you create time for yourself, you free up time to spend doing things you care about. You gain time to spend on your personal development and ultimately increase your quality of life. In the process, you learn to love yourself more. As you love yourself, you increase your ability to love others. It has been my own experience and that of many of my clients that internal work has improved relationships with spouses and loved ones.

Summary

Creating time for yourself is an important step towards your personal growth. Make time for yourself to complete the exercises in this book, time to relax and do things which are fulfilling for you and restore your energy.

In this chapter, you have considered how you spend your time today and how you want to spend your time. You have learned how to train yourself to listen to your heart's desire and say "No" whenever necessary.

Commit to creating time for yourself. If you haven't already, schedule a time in your calendar when you will go through the exercises in this chapter. Practice answering at least one request with a, "No" during the next week. Make sure to write this in your journal as a success.

Lotte's Strategies to Increase Your Quality of Life:

✔ Take time to create a "don't do" list.

✔ Say "No" at least once over the next week.

✔ Get in the habit of saying "No."

✔ Set aside a least one hour every week to spend doing things you love.

✔ Create time for yourself every week to keep working on your own personal development.

✔ You might need an outer commitment to support you in creating time for yourself. You can sign up for a weekly training or exercise activity that you would love to start doing.

✔ Taking a weekend off occasionally, to spend time alone or with loved ones provides a nice break to wind down. You can spend time relaxing away from home or on a workshop doing something completely different from what you usually do.

Chapter 10

Tap to Release

"Don't use the past to build a dam between you and the future."

WAEL EL-MANZALAWY

"I'm so afraid, what if I fail? What if they laugh at me?"

As we continued tapping, Pat's facial expression slowly became calmer. When her jaws relaxed, we ended the tapping sequence with a round of positive affirmations. "I believe I can sleep tonight," Pat spontaneously exclaimed as we completed the sequence. "I no longer feel anxiety as I think about my presentation tomorrow."

Emotional Freedom Technique (EFT), also known as "tapping" is one tool I usually teach my clients as a self-help tool. For about half of my clients, this is the tool they use most when they start to feel emotions arise. In this chapter, you will be introduced to the tapping technique.

Tapping is great when working from an outside-in perspective. When you are feeling emotions or limiting beliefs rising, you can tap on them to keep them in check. It is quick and easy to use and works on a variety of issues from anxiety to lack of concentration. Tapping can be done anywhere and anytime. However, most of my clients prefer to find a quiet place where they can be undisturbed for a few minutes.

How Tapping Works

Before I explain how to tap, let us explore how tapping works as a tool to heal. Tapping is using something called acupressure where you tap lightly on specific energy points. The energy points are the same as used in acupuncture, but tapping doesn't require any needles. While tapping, you state some clarifying words out loud or in your own mind. It sounds and is deceptively simple. Yet it is a very powerful technique, especially when an issue rises to the surface and you want to work on it right away.

One of the core reasons tapping works so well is it addresses the fear, doubt, unworthiness, or any other emotion rising within you. These negative emotions can be considered "stuck" energy. Going through a day, we experience many different feelings both negative and positive. This is healthy, as long as we allow these emotions to flow freely. When they are blocked, they get stuck in our body and can create both mental and physical issues. With tapping, you unlock these stuck emotions.

Tapping is a great self-help tool when you have something specific to work on. This means whenever you are feeling anxiety or self-doubt rise to the surface, it gives you a tip what to tap on. For example, you might feel, "I am so afraid I will show my lack of confidence at the meeting today." When using tapping, it is essential to tap on the *negative*. You want to remove the blockage caused by this negative feeling and let your emotions start flowing freely again.

Clients often ask me, "Why tap on the negative? Wouldn't it be better just to tap on the positive emotions we want to create?"

Looking for the positive in your life is generally healthy. Yet, there is also a negative side to it. If you are *forcing* yourself to think positively, suppressing the negative emotions, it is like putting a smiling mask over your face to hide your tears. When you tap on your negative emotions like anxiety, fear, limiting beliefs, or anger that surface for you, you allow them to flow and deal with them in a positive way.

The more you work on yourself, the more you will become aware of your reactions in any given situation. This applies to both your negative and positive emotions. This awareness helps you to move forward. Emotions you are aware of are workable emotions; the more you practice and learn the skills to work with them, the easier it becomes. This is especially important when you work with yourself without support from a therapist.

Lotte's Tip

Get in the habit of carrying a little notebook with you. Any time you become aware of a limiting belief and/or negative emotion, write it down. Especially if you don't have the option to work on it at that moment. Before going to bed, set time aside to go through your list. Recall the emotions and limiting beliefs and tap on them. You will be amazed how much better you will sleep and the progress you will make in your life.

Below are some of the issues I have worked on with clients of mine. This is intended to give you an idea of what you can work on using tapping.

- Anxiety

- Fear of speaking

- Sleeping disorder

- Sadness

- Weight problems

- Cravings

- Addictions

- Interactions with coworkers, boss, customers

- Self-belief issues

- Trust issues

I could continue, but I think you get the point. Tapping works great on a lot of different issues. I encourage you to experiment with the technique.

Now let's get into action.

The Procedure of Tapping

"I have been sleeping so badly lately," a client of mine complained as we started our session. "The customer has been blaming me even though I complete the job on time, and I keep thinking about it when I want to go to sleep."

Delving deeper into the story, it turned out my client was primarily angry that she felt ashamed because the client complained to her boss. And she felt deeply hurt because she knew she had delivered the promised work. It was time to tap.

Tapping Technique

The tapping method consists of four steps:

- **Initial measuring** how you are feeling initially around your issue. This will give you the ability to recognize your progress. Measure on a scale from 1 (not feeling anything) to 10 (feeling it acutely). What number pops into your head right now?

- Your **set-up statement**. This is working line you use to start your tapping sequence. You start by saying your set-up statement three times out loud or inside your head as you repeatedly tap lightly on the "karate chop point" with the fingertips of four fingers on the other hand. This point is located at the side of the hand below the little finger – the part of the hand you would use to split bricks with a karate chop. See Figure 1.

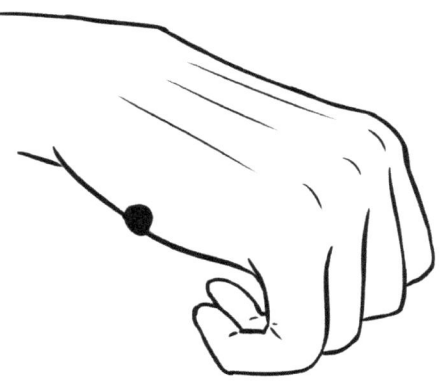

Figure 1. *The karate chop point*

As you tap, you repeat your set-up statement. A simple yet powerful set-up statement you can use by simply filling in the blank is this:

Even though I _____ , I fully and completely love and accept myself.

If it initially feels too difficult to say you love yourself, you can choose to use, "I choose to accept myself fully and completely," instead.

Some examples that you can use to fill out the blank is

- Even though I feel this anxiety, I…

- Even though I am afraid, I can't fall asleep, I…

- Even though I am scared I will fail this test, I…

- Even though I don't like being among too many people, I…

- Even though I am afraid to speak up, I…

After you have said your setup statement 3 times, you start doing the tapping rounds.

Tapping rounds. Every tapping sequence consists of a series of tapping rounds after the set-up statement is completed. Typically, one to five rounds is sufficient. During a round, you will tap repeatedly on each of the tapping points in sequence. You start on the eyebrow point, and from here you move to the side of the eye, under the eye, under the nose, the chin, the collarbone, under the arm and top of the head. See Figure 2.

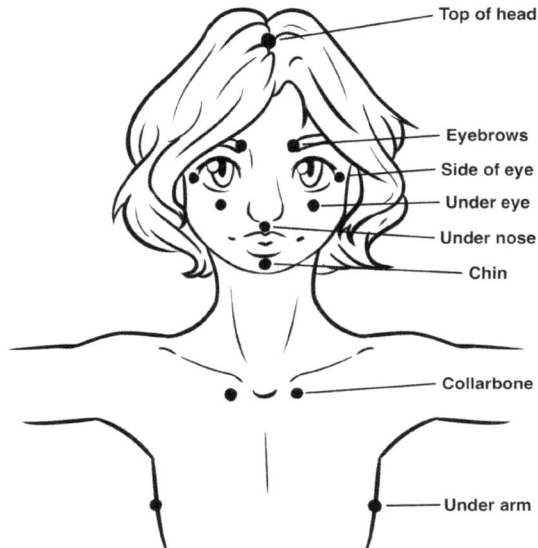

Figure 2. *The tapping points*

You tap using one or two fingers, tapping lightly on each point. As you tap on each point, you repeat the main issue that you are tapping on. Using the examples above, your tapping statement could sound like this:

- I feel this anxiety

- I am afraid I can't fall asleep

- I am scared I will fail this test

- I don't like being among too many people

- I am afraid to speak up

Note that you tap on the negative issue to set the negative energy free. As you use the tapping technique, you will often notice that just opening up for the negative energy and allowing it to flow freely, you will take a huge step forward.

- **Final measuring**. When you have completed a series of rounds, take a deep breath in, exhale and let go of any tension you are feeling in your body. Go back to your original statement and measure how you are feeling now.

Be as exact as you can when creating your tapping statements. Also, know that this takes practice. Like many of the other techniques I present in this book, there is no bad tapping. There is only good, better, and best tapping.

I know tapping might look complicated when explained in writing like this, but it really isn't difficult. To provide another way for you to learn tapping, I have produced a tapping video and placed it on the book website www.lifeafterbullying.com.

Anger Tapping Example

In the example with my client who was experiencing anger, the tapping procedure could look like this:

- Start by locating a feeling of anger in your body and measure it on a scale from 1 – 10, with 10 being most severe and 1 almost not an issue.

- Start tapping on the karate point. If you are right-handed, tap with your right hand on the karate point on the left hand (see figure figure 1). If you are left-handed, do it the other way around.

- Say your set-up statement and repeat three times. The set-up statement in the case could be "Even though I feel this anger, I choose to love and accept myself fully and completely."

- Now tap on the different acupuncture points as shown in figure 2. As you tap, repeat the key words: "I have this anger." Tap three rounds.

- State the key issue again and check on a scale from 1 – 10 how it feels now. Notice how much it has improved.

- Repeat if necessary. The goal is to get the number all the way down to three or lower.

Tapping Beyond the Immediate Feeling

In the example above, tapping on the feeling of anger is good. However, it is possible to get even quicker results if you can determine the reason behind the immediate feeling. In this case, what is the feeling that causes the anger?

A method for improving the efficiency of your tapping is to be aware of the feelings that come up while you tap. Write them down and then do another round of tapping on this new feeling when you have completed the first tapping rounds.

In this case, we discussed why my client was feeling the anger and what situation triggered it in her. We discovered that part of the problem was she was getting blamed for shoddy work by other people. She also felt ashamed and hurt due to the way this whole episode had come about. Finally, she had kept the shame and anger to herself instead of speaking up and sharing her point of view.

We tapped on the two statements "even though I feel hurt, I choose to deeply and completely love and accept myself" and "even though I feel ashamed, I choose to deeply and completely love and accept myself."

Her anxiety level went from an eight to a two. When I followed up a week later, the client told me she had slept better and had been able to speak up about the issue to her boss who supported her completely.

Lotte's Tip

Sometimes when you start tapping, your body feels the issue more acutely. It feels like your body is telling you, "Thank you for noticing me – now I will reveal just how severe it really is." Don't worry about this. Your body is simply fully revealing the feeling that is already stored in your body. Thank your body for giving you permission to work on it. Keep tapping, and in a few rounds, you will start to feel the benefit.

Standing Up for Yourself

It was my personal experience that I had a tough time speaking up. I have also seen again and again working with clients that people who have been deeply hurt in the past have trouble speaking up.

In this case, my client felt good after tapping on feelings of hurt and shame. In other cases, we might have done some tapping on the issues around "not speaking up."

Where are you not speaking up? Are there places where you know it would be healthy to speak up? Tap on it and explore what happens.

Everyday Tapping

Basic tapping doesn't take a long time to do. I often tell my clients a restroom is a very private place if you feel anxiety while being with other people. Just excuse yourself for a moment and make a trip to the bathroom where you can quickly and easily lower your anxiety level.

You can download the "tap along" MP3 audio file from my website and put it on your phone, so you always have it available.

A Positive Finish

When the anxiety level reduces to a value of two or three, you can start to tap on a positive feeling or the benefits you want to gain. This is optional; merely tapping on the negative emotion will give you a lot of benefits.

It can sometimes be hard to move from the negative to the positive statements. When I started tapping, this was a significant challenge for me. To make the shift to a positive statement easier, I have found the "choice" method helps.

In the choice method, you use the words, "I choose to." This emphasizes that you have the power to change the negative belief.

Choice Method Example

Let me give a personal example of a situation where I used a positive finish and the choice method in my own life. I have always had a hard time falling asleep when I miss my usual bedtime, and that anxiety still occasionally pops up when I come home late.

I use tapping to address this, and it works. In my case, my positive choice is to believe that I can fall at sleep in 10 minutes.

- My set-up statement would sound like this, "Even though I am afraid I can't fall asleep, I choose to love and accept myself fully and completely." Remember to say this statement three times.

- The first two to three tapping rounds focus on the negative emotion I want to dissolve, using the words, "I am afraid I can't fall asleep."

- When my intensity measurement shows the feeling being reduced to a two or three, I start the positive finish using the choice method. In the next tapping round, I use the sentence, "I choose to believe I can fall asleep during the next 10 minutes."

- Finally, you do one last tapping round alternating the negative and the positive statements. This will sound like this:

  - Eyebrow point: "I am afraid I can't fall asleep."

  - The side of the eye: "I choose to believe I can fall asleep during the next 10 minutes."

  - Under the eye: "I am afraid I can't fall asleep."

  - Under the nose: "I choose to believe I can fall asleep during the next 10 minutes."

  - Chin: "I am afraid I can't fall asleep."

  - Collarbone: "I choose to believe I can fall asleep during the next 10 minutes."

  - Under the arm: "I am afraid I can't fall asleep."

  - Top of the head: "I choose to believe I can fall asleep during the next 10 minutes."

Here are some more examples of negative emotions and their positive counterpart:

- I feel this anxiety – I choose to believe I can feel free

- I am scared I will fail this test – I choose to believe I can pass this test

- I don't like being among too many people – I choose to feel at peace at the party

- I am afraid to speak up – I choose to feel secure when I speak up

The Power of Tapping

As you already know, it can be a lot easier to make a rational argument about what we deserve than to believe it in our hearts. However, the heart is the key to a profound change and a place where I always find intense blocks when working with clients in one-on-one sessions.

As you use tapping regularly, you will also start shifting your internal beliefs. To keep track, remember to journal and notice the small changes.

When you don't feel good about yourself, it can be challenging to move into the more positive feelings like, "I can have friends," "I can get this promotion," or, "I can speak up."

Realize you do have a choice and a shift *is* possible. The choice method supports you in this. Every time you state your conscious *decision* to believe a positive thought, you improve your control over your own life. It might take a while, but slowly and steadily the shift to genuinely accepting you have a choice will happen.

> **Lotte's Tip**
>
> Play with the tapping method. Use it whenever you get the inspiration, "Maybe I can tap on this?" As you play with it, note the difference you feel. Success creates more success and tapping will become one of your tools.

Summary

Tapping is an excellent tool for you to have in your toolbox. Tapping can be used as often as you want and especially shines when you have something tangible to work on. Tapping works well on anxiety, speaking, sleeping issues, feeling low, blaming yourself, and many other feelings.

Lotte's Strategies to Increase Your Quality of Life

- ✓ No issue is too small to tap on. The more you tap, the more you release stuck emotions.

- ✓ Carry a notebook and write down whatever pops up during the day.

- ✓ Create time each day where you give yourself permission to release. Look at your notes and tap to release any negative feelings.

Chapter 11

Regenerating Images in Memory (RIM)

"What you feel is what you get, regardless of what you think."

DEBORAH SANDELLA

All the tools in *Life After Bullying* work well, but one stands out as exceptionally powerful to access the deep roots of hidden traumatic experiences: the RIM method developed by Dr. Deborah Sandella. RIM stands for Regenerating Images in Memory and is a process where we trust our own body's knowing. Let me give an example of RIM from my own practice.

During a workshop Carina broke down in tears when she tried to voice the statement, "I can." To uncover what was behind the upwelling emotions, I gently guided Carina to close her eyes and move into her body through her tears. As she sensed her body, a black cloud filling her whole chest drew her attention. When I asked Carina for someone or something to be with her to support her and create safety, an image of an old friend showed up. Confirming that she now felt safe, I guided her to imagine being in the black space, where an image of her father showed up.

Guiding Carina to express her feelings to her dad, she started to voice her distress as she felt it in that moment. "What I want to say to you, Dad, is that it felt like you were always scowling at me. I could never do anything right. It hurt me so much. It was like my brother could do anything, and I could do nothing right. It made me believe that I couldn't do anything and that is still following me today, I still believe that I can't do anything right. It made me believe that I am just a stupid little girl. I never felt loved by you Dad, and that really hurt."

When Carina had expressed all her hurt feelings, she moved her attention over to her Dad, looking from his eyes over at Carina, and expressed what he had received from her. "Carina, what I hear you say is that I was always scowling at you, always making you feel that you couldn't do anything right. That I made you feel like I didn't love you. Carina, I am so sorry to hear this, I never realized that you felt this way. I guess I didn't know how to support you the right way. I want you to know that I am so proud of you, of what you have achieved. And I love you so much."

Carina now moved back into her own body, receiving her dad's love and pride as colorful energy moving directly into her chest. The black cloud disappeared, and Carina felt light and started to own a belief that she is good enough and that she can do whatever she sets her mind to do.

How RIM Works

Hurt, anger, sadness, grief, joy, happiness. Whatever emotion we are experiencing in any given moment is a reaction to what is happening at the same time. Our emotions flow through us as water flows in a river. When we allow the emotion to be experienced and processed, it flows freely. When we don't want to experience the emotion, for example if it feels unsafe, we create an internal block like a dam in the river. Dr. Deborah Sandella has described the process in more detail in her book *Goodbye Hurt & Pain.*

When an event happens the body perceives as traumatic occurs, and is resisted, the emotions connected to the event get stuck and increase the intensity of that memory. These stuck emotions are later reactivated by flashbacks, intense body reactions, etc. The subconscious mind reacts to protect you from getting hurt again. Unfortunately, this often happens in a way that doesn't support us in our everyday life.

In Carina's situation, she never felt loved by her dad. On an unconscious level, his actions towards her made her believe she wasn't good at anything. In a child, this kind of message anchors in the young brain and prevents the child from living his or her life fully. Later in life, this belief can create stress, anxiety, depression, and other ailments. Because the RIM method keeps the rational left brain in service to the imagination of the creative right brain to create a whole brain process, it produces beneficial results without requiring or involving logical thinking. Carina was not consciously aware of how her father's scowling at her had made her believe she couldn't do anything right, but afterward, she felt empowered and concluded, "I **can** create success in my business."

As a RIM facilitator, I guide my clients to unlock the answers within them. As my clients gain new insights and trust in their own abilities, a new emotional memory can then be created. In the process, we trust and follow whatever comes up, knowing whatever shows up is there for a reason. In a relaxed state, clients are guided to listen to their body, images, and feelings from actual or imagined memory. Because we follow the organic process, the client cannot do the process wrong. Later in this chapter, you find an exercise you can use to uncover hidden blocks, created when you were unable to express your emotions through your voice.

In RIM, the feeling of having someone loving there with you is essential. Just think about a situation where you have hurt yourself, maybe as a child, and someone held you as you cried or comforted you as they cleaned up the wound. Being supported allows the expression of our emotions to be safe.

Gaining New Insight Through Your Virtual Resource

One day, while I was still working as an occupational therapist, my patient Helene said to me: "Lotte, when you are not here, I feel like I

have a little copy of you sitting on my shoulder. And when I get stuck,
I just ask you what to do, and you always help by telling me what the
next step is."

As an occupational therapist, I was used to supporting people with cognitive brain damage in many different ways. This was a new response, however, and I didn't quite know what to make of Helene's description. And yet this client had apparently found a way of coping with her severe memory loss. She was finding the answers she needed by asking her imaginary copy of me and listening to the answers "I" provided.

When I later received my training in the RIM technique, it all made perfect sense. In RIM, we use a virtual resource to create safety and gain new insights. Feeling safe is very important to remove our internal blocks. Having someone you can trust on a deep level with you creates an internal shift in the way we handle traumatic stuck memories. Even when this virtual resource is in our memory, our body still perceives it as safe.

Whenever you are feeling stuck and want to gain new insights, a supportive virtual resource is called upon. This virtual resource can be anything from a beloved animal, a deceased wise ancestor, a mentor, a spiritual guide or something in nature. Jane, a client of mine with a very untrusting childhood, was unable to find anybody from her childhood. There was nobody to protect her while she grew up. When I invited her to look for something in nature, immediately a big evergreen pine showed up. Jane realized that she always felt at peace when walking in the forest. Feeling the branches holding her, Jane was safe enough to be able to speak her deepest hurt. Afterward, Jane felt an inner peace and gained the confidence to increase her quality of life.

Twisting in pain, I listened to the people next to me describing how relaxed they felt after the meditation. All I could feel were two massive imaginary spikes stabbing into my shoulders.

This was when Dr. Deborah Sandella, the founder of the RIM technique, took me aside and guided me through my first RIM session. With the support of my late grandmother as a virtual resource, I was guided to move my awareness into the spikes, and I sensed an image of myself at the age of seven. When I moved into the image of the 7-year-old me, I sensed how I was standing against the wall at the back of the class, facing towards the class. As I looked out of my 7-year-old eyes, I saw an image of my teacher pointing at me with the whole class laughing.

Feeling my grandmother's supportive hands on my shoulders, I looked directly at my teacher and was guided to voice my hurt and frustration: "Why are you laughing at me? It hurt so much. This way I will never be able to learn, I will always feel stupid and awkward. How do you think I can learn anything if I must always be afraid that you will laugh at me? This whole thing makes me just want to run away."

As I kept voicing my internal pain, I could sense how the pain in my shoulders was getting less and less intense. As I had expressed everything that was present, my grandmother began to speak. As I moved my awareness over to my grandmother, I could feel her pain and love for me, her granddaughter.

Spontaneously words appeared in my awareness to speak to Lotte: "Lotte, it is terrible what happened to you and yet it has nothing to do with you. Let your teacher fight her own demons." Looking me directly in the eyes, my grandmother continued: "Lotte I want you to know you are strong, worthy and capable of learning and of creating a happy life for yourself and your family. Lotte, it is time to let go and move forward, and I will always be here to support you."

Moving my awareness back into 7-year-old Lotte, I could look back over at the image of my grandmother. I was able to feel all the words that had been spoken coming into me as a stream of colored energy that came in through my shoulders and spread out through my whole body. My shoulders once again felt relaxed, and it felt like a huge weight had been lifted off.

Feeling the internal safety from my grandmother gave me the ability to voice my embodied pain in a way where I felt very supported and had permission to speak whatever was present – even hate and anger. Saying all of this and then listening to the supportive words from my grandmother permanently shifted how I perceived the memory. From then on, I was hooked on the process and started to take all the education I could get. Today, RIM is a big part of my one-on-one work with clients.

One way to release an inner block is to give it a voice. Holding back and not speaking up can create stuck emotions. Giving these stuck emotions a voice releases the block, and you can generate new insights along the way. The next exercise is one you can do yourself to gain a new awareness of where you silence your voice, allowing you to speak up and release the internal block.

Exercise 23: Enhance Your Voice

This is one of the official RIM exercises that I share with you with the permission of Dr. Deborah Sandella, who founded the RIM technique. It first appeared in her book *Goodbye Hurt and Pain*. You can find more information on the RIM technique on the book website.

1. Rest in a comfortable space with your eyes closed. Focus on your breath, taking several deep, comforting breaths, inhaling deeply through your nose, and exhaling slowly through your mouth.

2. As you feel more relaxed, sense in your body where your voice is hiding, and notice the location, size, shape, and color. You might get a specific image or just a sense of knowing. Anything is welcome. Take as much time as you need.

3. As you sense this, ask your imagination to bring in a virtual resource to travel with you. Welcome in whoever or whatever shows up and feel how you are now supported.

4. With your virtual resource, move into the energy of what has called upon your attention. As you settle in, ask your imagination to call up a number. Openly receive this number as your age when you first felt this way.

5. An image of yourself at this age appears.

6. Imagine being this younger self. Look out of these younger eyes and see who silenced your voice.

7. With your virtual resource acting as a safe force field between you and this person, safely speak or write what wants to be expressed to this person that has never been voiced before. Continue expressing, "what I want to say to you that I have never said before..." Take whatever time needed.

8. Continue to speak until you are loudly and clearly sharing your voice. Stretch into it. Take as much time as you want or need.

9. Notice how this feels in your body.

10. Find in your body the new feeling of expressing yourself in a clear, loud voice. Notice its location, color, and texture.

11. Moving into it, immerse yourself in this, "expressing your voice" energy, as you swim in it, play in it, and become it.

12. Notice how this feel.

---

13. When you are ready, open your eyes and record your experience in your journal. You can also share it with someone, noting what you learned and how it can help you in your current life.

Well done. You can keep doing this exercise over and over. Each time, you will get new insights and release another level.

Summary

Old emotional experiences can be deeply anchored in your body. Especially as young children, we perceive experiences very intensely, and they can have a lasting impact. RIM is a method to uncover your hidden limiting beliefs, work through these beliefs, and create a new empowering understanding. Feeling the loving support of someone at your side gives you the safety and ability to unlock and recreate your memory

Lotte's Strategies to Increase Your Quality of Life

✔ Be open to examining your past, uncovering the traumatic experiences, and re-imagining them.

✔ Go through the RIM exercise to enhance your voice several times. Accept whatever reveals itself and recreate the memory that shows up.

✔ Listen to the recorded RIM meditation.

Chapter 12

Breathe and Let Go

"Only I can change my life. No one can do it for me."

CAROL BURNETT

The crisis team was overwhelmed. Contradictory messages kept pouring in, and we were struggling to keep a clear picture of the situation. I took a deep breath in. As I slowly exhaled, I noticed how I relaxed. "Is anyone missing?" I calmly asked. As we continued the exercise among the first responders in the trauma support group, I was continuously aware of how a simple act of deep breathing had a profound impact on my ability to remain calm.

Deep relaxation, meditation, and mindfulness have long been proven to calm our nervous system. It helps with disorders like anxiety, depression, and stress. The secret is that our body can't be both tense and relaxed at the same time.

Whenever you feel any level of anxiety, distrust, sadness or similar feelings, it is normal to tighten up and feel your muscles tense. This again signals your brain that you are in a stressful situation and need to prepare to fight or flee. Your breathing gets shallower and quicker.

When the sympathetic nervous system responds to stress and fear, it rapidly releases a series of stress chemicals into our bloodstreams. These include cortisol, adrenaline, and noradrenaline. This reaction happens almost instantaneously but shutting down the system takes more time. When you are always on guard, your body reacts by staying in a state of alert. This again can cause sleeping issues, weight gain, increased anxiety and depression, cognitive problems, and many other ailments.

In the same way tension in your muscles creates a stress reaction in your body, you can trick your body into relaxing. Try right now: Close your eyes, if you are in a safe place, or just focus on a spot in front of you and notice your breathing. As you exhale, empty your lungs completely, and then take in one long deep breath. Now take a few relaxed, deep breaths, making each as long as it feels comfortable. As your breathing slows down, notice the difference in your body. Your body quickly becomes more relaxed.

When you relax, you allow the parasympathetic nervous system to rest, and your body goes back to a state of calmness. As you relax, you enhance chemicals like GABA (which makes you feel calm), endorphins (which make you feel good and lessen pain), and serotonin (which has a significant impact on our mood and overall state of wellbeing).

Besides calming your mind and body in the moment, practicing different relaxation techniques have a long-term effect. They support you to be calmer in any stressful situation and bounce back from stress to relaxation more quickly.

Moving into Relaxation

"I can't meditate," and, "My mind keeps churning," are the two most common objections I hear when I work with clients and introduce the importance of relaxation. Here, I will address both of these. If you took a few deep breaths described earlier, you have already experienced how you can easily relax your body. This simple act of focusing on your breathing can get you back into a relaxed state at any time. In the next exercise, we expand this breathing technique a little more.

Exercise 24: Breathing to Relax

This relaxation exercise can be done anytime with closed or open eyes. In the beginning, it might be easier for you to close your eyes, but if you aren't in a position where this feels right or is safe, simply allowing your gaze to soften works fine as well. Straighten your back and raise your head so that your whole spine is straight. This expands your chest area and allows you to take deeper breaths. You can do this relaxing breathing for as long as you like.

- Look ahead with a straight back.

- Start focusing on your breathing.

- Close your eyes, if you are in a position where you can do this.

- Follow the flow of your breath – in through your nostrils and out through your mouth.

- Now slowly allow your breath to go deeper into your body. Feel how it flows in through your nostrils, down to your lungs and pushes down your diaphragm.

- As you exhale, open your mouth a little and feel the air on your lips as you empty your lungs.

- Take another slow, deep breath in, allowing it to fill your lungs completely.

- Keep following your breaths for a few more in- and exhales. Notice how your body becomes more relaxed.

- When you are ready to return, take one more deep breath and roll your shoulders as you exhale and open your eyes.

How do you feel? This is an elementary exercise that you can do anytime and everywhere when you want to relax a little more.

> **Lotte's Tip: Enhance Your Focus with Mindfulness**
>
> You can use this breathing technique to be more mindful and focused on an upcoming task. It doesn't matter if you want to clarify your goals, play a game with your kids, cook dinner, or work on a business report. This technique enhances your focus for all tasks. Just get ready to start the task, then follow the breathing exercise described above for a few deep breaths.
>
> Before you return, make a mental statement to set your intention for what you want to create or experience. For example: "For the next half hour I will be fully engaged in playing this game with my kids and enjoy the experience." Or, "For the next half hour, I will work fully concentrated on completing this report."

Relaxing and Letting Go

"My head keeps spinning, I get stuck in my thoughts." It is easy to beat yourself up, but the reality is that thoughts come and go on their own for everyone. The problem happens only when we actively try to push our thoughts away; the more we push, the more we struggle with the thought. In my early days as an occupational therapist in rehabilitation, I learned a technique that has served me well ever since. The following story illustrates this technique.

Anna was fighting to complete the task of putting on her clothes. Despite her challenges, Anna didn't want any support. She was one-hundred-percent sure that there was nothing wrong with her. Anna kept complaining, and her behavior seemed like that of a little child. Taking a deep breath in, I mentally went into my inner office and pulled out a drawer reserved for this specific task. In the drawer was only one item, a big piece of paper with the words "They can't help it." As I closed the drawer, I took a deep breath in and felt how my tension faded away, and I was once again able to give my full attention to supporting Anna.

Yes, Anna and others with cognitive dysfunctions can't help reacting the way they do. Intellectually, therapists know this. However, unless we use mental techniques like this, we are at risk of suboptimal instinctive reactions.

As I went through my own growth process, I realized this mental technique was handy to ease my own internal struggle. Whenever I felt limiting thoughts or internal tension in a situation, I reduced it by my own variation of the drawer exercise. I would simply welcome the thought, thank it for showing up, and then place it in the drawer "just for now. " I have found that using the words, "Just for now," supports me in setting the thoughts aside. I am not disallowing this thought, simply letting it go for the time being.

It is important not to push the thoughts away, trying to put a mental lid on it. Instead, allow the thought to come into your awareness, acknowledge it for showing up, and then simply put it aside just for now. Sometimes, this simple exercise repeated a few times is all it takes. At other times, you might need to work harder on your thoughts using one of the other tools.

Exercise 25: Release Your Thoughts

When you become aware of the thoughts that show up, practice welcoming the thought to set it aside, just for now. The following exercise guides you through the steps. Feel free to do several rounds of the exercise, letting go a little more each time.

I want to point out two things about this exercise. First: never try to press the thought back down. The more pressure you put on it, the more it struggles to come up to your awareness. Second: using "just for now" makes it easier to set the thought aside. Otherwise, you often create an internal conflict where your mind is waiting for the thought to come back.

- Notice any thought that shows up.

- Take a deep breath and relax just a little as you exhale.

- Welcome the thought as best you can right now without judging it.

- Choose to mentally thank the thought for bringing the message to your awareness.

- Mentally put the thought aside, just for now, by placing the thought in a mental drawer. Gently say to the thought: "Thank you for showing up. I don't have time right now, so I choose to put you aside just for now."

- Keep following your breaths for a few more in- and exhales and notice how your body becomes more relaxed.

Internal tension can be handled in the same way. You just replace the word "thought" with the word "tension" or name the specific kind of tension.

Play around with a mental picture that works for you. Some of my clients have been creating several drawers or shelves in their mental storage room, so that thoughts that belong together can be placed together. Others have visualized fluffy white clouds passing by, set their thoughts on the clouds and then sensed them drifting away.

Harvest the Benefits of Meditation

A higher level of energy in the evening and improved sleep are the two direct benefits that support me in keeping a daily habit of meditation between 10 – 30 minutes each afternoon. Long-term benefits for me include an ability to stay calmer in stressful situations, and better focus on my work.

An excellent and easy meditation for any length of time can be done by just combining the two exercises above: "Focus on Your Breathing" and "Release Your Thoughts." By combining these two exercises, you allow your body to go deeper into the meditation.

Remember that meditation is not necessarily an absence of thoughts, even though that can happen. It is merely noticing without judging what is present and letting this flow through you.

Exercise 26: Relax and Let Go

In this exercise, you will be combining the two exercises above. You focus on your breath and at the same time allow your thoughts to flow through you and out.

- Look ahead with a straight back.

- Start focusing on your breathing.

- Follow the flow of your breath in through your nostrils and out through your mouth.

- Now slowly allow your breath to go deeper into your body. Feel how it flows into your lungs and push down your diaphragm.

- Keep following your breath as it flows in through the nostrils, filling up your lungs, and slowly exhale out through your mouth. In and out, for the rest of your meditation.

- When it feels comfortable, close your eyes

- Whenever you become aware of a thought, simply welcome the thought as best you can right now without judging it.

- Choose to mentally thank the thought for bringing the message to your awareness.

- Now, mentally put the thought aside, just for now, by placing the thought in a mental drawer, on a shelf or on a fluffy white cloud that is passing by in your mind's eye.

- Gently say to the thought: "Thank you for showing up. I don't have time right now, so I choose to put you aside just for now."

- Return to following your breaths.

- When you are ready to end the meditation, take one very deep breath in. As you exhale, gently bring your awareness back into the room and open your eyes.

- Rub your hands together palm to palm until they feel warm and gently massage your face.

Meditation is not a quick fix. Its power lies in slowly increasing your health and wellbeing. At some point, you might experience being calm in a situation where you would usually feel stressed. Or you will notice how you wake up in the morning feeling energized and realizing you had a great night's sleep.

Getting into the habit of meditating between 10 and 30 minutes a day improves your health and wellbeing. I invite you to experience with meditation by giving yourself permission take one month where you meditate each day for at least 10 minutes. Feel free to play some relaxing music as you meditate.

Summary

Relaxation improves your health and wellbeing. You can't be stressed and relaxed at the same time. Even just a few deep breaths can calm you and make you more relaxed to continue whatever you are doing. Spending a few minutes to meditate on a regular basis is beneficial. Some of the benefits are improved sleep, reduced stress, enhanced energy, and less anxiety.

Lotte's Strategies to Increase Your Quality of Life

- ✔ Pause during the day and take a few deep breaths in and out. Notice how you relax.

- ✔ Take the challenge and practice meditation for one month with a minimum of 10 minutes a day. You might realize how beneficial it is and want to continue.

- ✔ Before starting a new task, take a few deep breaths and state to yourself your intention for the period of time.

- ✔ Start becoming aware of your thoughts. Allow yourself to welcome any disempowering thought and set it aside "just for now."

Chapter 13

Expand Your Comfort Zone

"Whenever you feel uncomfortable, instead of retreating back into your old comfort zone, pat yourself on the back and say, 'I must be growing,' and continue moving forward."

T. HARV EKER

I took a deep breath and let everything I knew go. I walked through Security to take the first step of my journey, knowing that there would be 20 hours of traveling before reaching my destination. I would have to deal with every person on the way on my own, find my way through foreign airports, finding a shuttle bus and checking in at the hotel. I had rarely traveled this far before and never alone. Every step would be a challenge. I prayed that nothing would go wrong and that I would arrive at my destination safely.

I was about to embark on a flight from Denmark to the United States. For the past months, the butterflies in my stomach had been growing steadily more agitated, and yet I knew I had to take this step. This was the next huge leap out of my comfort zone. I felt the urge to win over myself and move forward. For 15 years, I had been growing on my own in small steps, using self-study courses on cassette tapes and later CDs. Now I was ready to enter the next round of personal learning and growth.

You can compare your comfort zone to the walls of a house. It is easy to snuggle up inside the walls of your home, forgetting your fears and your discomfort by immersing yourself in television or a good book.

Personally, I would dive into a book that would help me forget the things that went on around me, especially my own fears and limiting beliefs. But nestling inside your house doesn't move you forward, and you might feel that life is moving past you without you living the life you truly want to live.

Your comfort zone is an invisible wall. Inside, everything feels safe and secure. When you move towards the wall, limiting beliefs and internal fears start to show up.

We all have a comfort zone that protects us from taking risks that can hurt us. Your comfort zone is created by your past experiences and is guided by your own limiting beliefs. A protection system is good, but it can also prevent you from moving forward and obtaining the life you want to live.

Stepping Outside Your Walls

Fortunately, our comfort zone is flexible. When you push forward and take a leap of faith for something you want, your comfort zone expands. When I moved to Germany, there were many small steps I took to move forward. I would talk to people at the playground even when I still spoke only rudimentary German. I would chat with people in our apartment building and everywhere else where I got the opportunity.

Taking small steps outside your comfort zone moves you forward. Interestingly, the more you go for it, the easier it gets and the bigger steps you take. You start to experience that the benefits are much more substantial than the fear and this accelerates you forward.

Lotte's Tip: Know the Benefit

Knowing the ultimate benefit of challenging yourself to move forward makes it easier to expand your comfort zone. To discover your internal drivers, reflect on the following questions. Write down the answer in your journal.

- How do you want to feel?
- How do you want to approach life?
- What do you want to be able to do?

No matter how far you want to move your comfort zone right now, the most significant step is to start. Every time you expand your comfort zone, you will be pushing through your own limiting beliefs and fears.

When you start to feel the fear and limiting beliefs, it is a sign that you are getting close to the edge of your comfort zone. This means you are about to grow, taking the next step towards the life you want. Congratulate yourself for taking the steps and push through.

One of the strongest reasons to expand your comfort zone is the personal reward you get. Be on the lookout for indications that prove how you have changed. You might not see the clue tomorrow, but at one point you will realize that some things you used to fear have suddenly become much less challenging – or even enjoyable. A pitfall that can sabotage your development if you are not aware of it is that we are more inclined to notice the things that limit us. When things become more natural, we no longer pay attention and might miss important signs that we have changed and grown.

> **Lotte's Tip: Notice Your Progress**
>
> When you write in your journal or do the mirror exercise, fill in the answer to the following question:
>
> What I realized was easier for me today than previously is
>
> _____
>
> Remember even the slightest progress is worth remembering and writing down in your journal.

Feel Your Fear and Do It Anyway

Having arrived safely at my hotel, I still had the most consequential step ahead of me. It took an enormous effort to open the door and step out of my room the next morning. I would be going to a conference room with 400 other people. Even though I felt the fear, I was also excited and ready because I genuinely wanted to expand and to move forward towards my dreams.

During the first days, I would slip back to my room to relax occasionally. I kept pushing outside my comfort zone, the fear slowly subsided, and I was able to engage in conversations with other participants.

My greatest success was on the last day when we were given the opportunity to acknowledge another person. One lady pointed at me, forcing me to stand up in front of everyone. Then she acknowledged how I had gone from very shy in the beginning to more open and relaxed with other people. I had tears in my eyes and was amazed that other people had noticed my challenges and growth.

The first few times you move outside your comfort zone in a specific area, it is likely to feel very uncomfortable pushing through your limiting beliefs and fears. Taking a deep breath and going for it anyway is the key. The next time you do the same thing, it will feel slightly easier. Every time you have taken a deep breath in and pushed your comfort zone, realize how you feel as you have taken the steps. And always remember to reward yourself and acknowledge that you did take this action.

When the goal becomes more important than the challenges to get there, you will feel the push to move outside your comfort zone. Look at the goals you created earlier. Are these the kinds of goals you want so much that you are ready to expand your comfort zone to achieve them? Or do they need a little makeover to be challenging enough to push your walls?

Pushing Your Walls

When you push yourself outside your comfort zone, you get rewarded in one way or another. It can be internally or externally. You never know how your rewards will come to you. Sometimes they come from being acknowledged by other people. At other times they come from noticing yourself how you thrive.

Feel and acknowledge your fear. Whenever you are taking the next step, your level of fear is an indicator of how far you are pushing outside your comfort zone. The further you push, the more you grow and expand. The fear wants to block you from moving forward. It is there to protect you from being hurt again. While well-meaning, this protection is also limiting your life, maybe so much that you don't like what you have become. Think of fear as an indicator that you are moving forward. When it gets too strong, and you are about to stop, you can ask yourself this question:

Would I rather keep feeling the way I feel today,
or would I rather push through this fear and expand my life?

As you keep moving through the fear that shows up in your body, remember your fear is telling you that you are taking the risks that will allow you to expand and move forward. I didn't believe I was good enough and thought I could not learn. Now I know that I *am* good enough. I know you also have a purpose with your life and a message to share with the world.

Lotte's Tip: Take Action to Push Your Walls

Pushing your limits will make you grow and expand. It will show you. You are good enough, and you are capable. You will discover you are knowledgeable and have a voice that needs to be heard.

What one small step can you take today to push yourself just a little? Write it down and set up time when you will do it.

_____

Make a habit of challenging yourself to push outside your comfort zone at least once a week – preferably more often. The steps don't have to be big. Every little thing you do where you feel the fear and do it anyway will be stretching your comfort zone.

Expanding Your Walls with the Tools in Your Toolbox

I reminded myself the worst thing that could happen was she might turn her back to me. I approached the other mother at the playground. Soon we were happily talking about our kids. Once again, I had taken a small step to expand my comfort zone, and again my fear was proven wrong.

As you experience your fear, remember there are several tools you can use to lessen the tension you are feeling. Three of the techniques at the beginning of Part Three are especially helpful to release the upwelling fear: "Tap to Release," "Regenerating Images in Memory (RIM)" and "Breathe and Let Go." I teach these processes to most of my clients to support them in handling their fear whenever it comes up. If you like, go back to these chapters to refresh your knowledge.

It's Not as Bad as You Think

My mentor Jack Canfield says that the word "fear" is really an acronym for

Fantasized Experiences Appearing Real

Recall a time when you did something you were afraid to do. This can be anything – from a rollercoaster ride to speaking in front of other people. As you recall the event, consider what happened. How were you feeling when you started doing this specific thing? In most cases, your fear disappears or lessens dramatically as you step into doing the particular thing you were fearful about.

It is almost always the case that when we choose to do something despite our fears, the experience is not as bad as we fear it to be. Our mind creates this massive feeling of fear to protect us, but to grow, we need to let go of this protective mechanism. As you move through your fear, you will typically overcome your fear even before you have completed the task.

Lotte's Tip: The Recipe for Success

The recipe for success has just four ingredients:

Decide on your next step

Feel the fear

Take action

Expand your life.

Keep making this recipe, and your life will expand to your dreams and beyond.

Action Plan

The following exercise is created to support you in moving outside your comfort zone. In the exercise, you will discover both the benefits from taking action and how you are likely to feel if you don't act. By considering both sides, you are both pushing and pulling yourself to act.

Exercise 27: Take a Step Outside Your Comfort Zone

Decide on one step you can take today to expand your comfort zone. You can pick something that moves you toward one of your goals, or another challenge you are facing.

What is the exact next step you can take, where you are currently feeling a level of fear? Write it down with as many details as possible. For example: "I will speak up at the next meeting with my coworkers and say what I honestly mean about the current challenge at work."

_____

_____

_____

How will you feel when you have taken this specific action? For example: "I will feel relieved, because I have wanted to say this for several weeks, but until now I have been too afraid to take action."

_____

_____

_____

What do you most fear will happen when you act? For example: "I fear that my coworkers will laugh at me and not acknowledge how I feel."

_____

_____

_____

What will happen if you do not act? For example: "I will keep feeling stressed about the current situation, be tenser at home, and I will feel like a bad mom"

_____

_____

_____

What is the best possible outcome from you acting? For example: "My coworkers acknowledge how I feel, and we work together to create a solution."

_____

_____

_____

It is important to think of the best outcome your action can make possible. How it will make you feel? Isn't that outcome worth taking action for? Are you ready to take this specific action? And win over yourself? I hope you are.

If you happen to feel this action is too big a challenge right now, feel free to redo the exercise with a more manageable task. Write your original action in your journal and take this action some other time. And remember: We tend to think only of the worst possible outcome, which expands the fear. The worst-case scenario almost never happens.

Summary

Our minds create our comfort zone to protect us from being hurt. It is constructed from past negative experiences. Often, this self-protection reaches a level that prevents us from moving forward and living the life we truly want to live. Expanding your comfort zone is the key to expanding your life.

Whenever you feel fear before moving into action, appreciate that this is a sign that you are about to expand your comfort zone. Feeling your fear and doing it anyway is the path to personal growth. Remember to consider the word fear as an acronym for Fantasized Experiences Appearing Real. Our worst fears almost never materialize in real life. As you practice expanding your comfort zone, you will learn the benefits and know that it is worth the fear.

Today I welcome the feeling of fear as an indicator I am stepping up to yet another challenge and am growing in the process. I invite you to start to *feel the fear and do it anyway* to move forward towards creating the life you want to live. And I trust that one day, you too will start welcoming your fear as a sign of growth.

Lotte's Strategies to Increase Your Quality of Life:

- ✔ Go through the exercise "Take a step outside your comfort zone" with several different steps you want to take. Make a small list of possible actions that will support you in moving forward.

- ✔ Remember to think of the word fear as an acronym for "Fantasied Experiences Appearing Real." Usually, the outcome you fear won't materialize. You are far more likely to experience a positive result.

- ✔ Use the different techniques to support you in working through your fears: Letting go, RIM, and tapping.

- ✔ Complete a 30-day challenge: Each day for 30 days, take a small step outside your comfort zone. It can be to smile at a stranger, give a co-worker a hug, or make a positive remark where you would usually have stayed silent.

Chapter 14

Physical Challenges and Personal Growth

"If we never experience the chill of a dark winter, it is very unlikely that we will ever cherish the warmth of a bright summer's day."

ANTHON ST. MAARTEN

The yellow helmet bounced down the mountain, jumping up and down till it finally came to rest between two rocks. From above it was just a tiny dot, hardly to be seen unless you knew where to look. The only problem was that it was my helmet, supposed to be on my head. Now I felt unprotected and was clinging to the mountainside, terrified to move.

I knew intellectually that the climbing rope secured me. But how do you tell that to your body when you are scared sick? I was lowered back down to the ledge. I stood there devastated – I had lost again.

Overcoming the Challenge

Back in 1989, my fiancé persuaded me to join him on an advanced hiking course. Part of this was a short mountain climb that served as an introduction to this art. While the climb itself was only 150 feet, it took place above a drop of 500 feet. Up until now, it had been a great trip. This was our third day hiking, carrying everything we needed for camping on our backs. And I had managed to keep up with the boys. At least up until now.

I had never been introduced to personal growth training nor had any experience in pushing myself beyond my comfort zone. I had yet to learn that when we push ourselves physically with an intense and emotional challenge, we strengthen ourselves mentally as well.

As I stood there, shaken and devastated, my fiancé encouraged me to try again, and I did not want to let him down. This was a strong emotional push for me. But how could I possibly do it? Then one of the instructors offered to climb up with me.

I took a long breath and accepted the challenge. It felt like the climb took forever, but every time fear paralyzed me, my instructor would point out the next move and handhold.

When we finally reached the top, a feeling of pure joy and a deep inner sense of worthiness and gratitude filled my whole body. I felt as though I was flying the rest of the day, not noticing my heavy backpack. Even today I can easily close my eyes and remember the feeling.

Getting the Right Support

Overcoming physical challenges can be an excellent tool for self-improvement. I know that for me, using physical challenges to push myself out of my comfort zone has worked wonders.

However, this tool often needs hands-on, physical support from someone else. If my climbing instructor had not been next to me, showing me where to place my hands and feet, I would have been lowered from the cliff face in defeat again.

Today, the internet makes it easy to find both individual instructors and support groups.

Some people prefer the privacy of working with a specific coach or guide to meet some challenge. When I recently took up kayaking, I found an experienced instructor nearby who offered a compact weekend course to get me started.

Others prefer the social element of meeting with others, whether for a run around the park or to plan a multi-day bike trip.

If you work at a company that offers physical teambuilding activities like a company running club or aerobics class, sign up and see if it is useful for you.

Benefits of Overcoming Physical Challenges

My experience climbing this rock wall in Sweden also taught me that overcoming a physical challenge outside your comfort zone provides lasting benefits. Some of them are:

- Improved self-confidence

- Expanded comfort zone

- Strengthened belief in yourself

- A positive feeling of having accomplished something special

There is a special effect from physical achievement that the mental and spiritual tools in this book only simulate or do not address: The physical embodiment of your progress.

Because you have used all your senses in the experience, the experience is anchored very deeply in your body and has a permanent effect. Winning physically over your own limiting beliefs and stretching yourself in the process opens you up for building new pathways in your brain. Achieving the goal means you create a strong positive memory that completely obliterates memories of the anxiety you might have felt along the way.

Taking up Your Challenge

What kind of physical activity will you choose to grow yourself? What comes to mind right now? Maybe you will sign up for an event you've heard of? Your activity could be something mundane like walking or jogging, or something exotic like scuba diving. Even a walk around the block can be a challenge for you if you are currently spending your time behind your own closed door. Write down what you want to do next to challenge yourself.

When you have chosen an activity, research what your opportunities are. If you have selected a type of activity, find an event or group near you. If you have chosen a specific event, find out what training or other preparation you will need, and who can help you with that. It might be an individual or a group.

Finally, get out your calendar and set a time when you will take the first step – calling a club, booking a coach or signing up for an event.

Lotte's Tip

All levels of exercise cause your brain to produce endorphins, which are natural opioids that put you in a better mood. Whenever you are feeling low, head out for some exercise. Even 10 minutes of brisk walking creates wonders.

Endorphins are released by doing any kind of physical activities, for example

- Walking, jogging, biking or swimming

- Team sports like basketball, soccer or handball

- Group activities like yoga, gymnastics or dancing

- Activities like cleaning or gardening

Next time you are cleaning your house, put on some uplifting music and take a few dance steps in the process. This can make cleaning much more enjoyable.

Summary

All kinds and levels of exercise release endorphins and are a great way to uplift your mood. When you challenge yourself physically outside your comfort zone, you will experience lasting personal growth. You enhance your self-confidence, expand your comfort zone, and strengthen your internal belief in yourself.

Lotte's Strategies to Increase Your Quality of Life

✔ Make it a habit to fit in some physical activities throughout your week to get a boost of natural endorphins.

✔ Challenge yourself outside your comfort zone with a physical activity, where you push your limits a little (or a lot).

✔ Use the techniques at the beginning of Part Three if you feel the urge to release inner tension as you challenge yourself: "Tap to Release," "Regenerating Images in Memory (RIM)," and "Breathe and let go."

Chapter 15

Learn from Your Life

"You are allowed to be both a masterpiece and a work in progress, simultaneously."

SOPHIA BUSH

"Oh, this is just a…" I stopped abruptly: I had just received a compliment for my dress, and as usual, I was well on my way to diminish it. Was it really a nothing special? Yes, the material was inexpensive, but I had also designed the dress myself, and it had the right shape and color for me. Wasn't it a piece that I deserved to be proud of?

"That was easy."

"Nothing to talk about."

"This is just an old dress."

Do you recognize a pattern? Do you fall victim to it, too? When was the last time you received a compliment? Did you accept it fully, or did you deflate it and in fact diminish both yourself and the giver of the compliment?

Receiving Positive Feedback

Being able to accept a compliment is healing. And it is beneficial both for you and for the person who is giving it to you from an honest heart.

Receiving a compliment is part of the external feedback the world provides for you. Notice any compliment you get and use it to support your change.

I know it can feel uncomfortable in the beginning. Start slowly by being open to receiving any positive remark you get. Take it in and welcome it as best you can with an open heart. Then thank the person that gave you the compliment. Do not make excuses or trivialize it. The person who gave you this compliment gave it because they believe it. I invite you to believe it too.

When you write in your journal at the end of the day, make sure to make a note of any compliment you received during the day. If you like, you can create a special page for this. This supports you in acknowledging and integrating the compliment one more time.

Positive feedback can also come indirectly. Questions like "How did you manage to do this…" is positive feedback. The silence when people are enjoying your food, intense listening or the smile from your college is also feedback. Take the time to savor the feeling and give yourself a mental pat on the back.

Discarding Useless Feedback

In life, we also receive negative feedback. There are two kinds: Useful and useless. This section is about how to discover and discard useless feedback, which is simply disguised aggression from another person. We'll return to how to handle useful feedback at the end of the chapter.

"Lady, a spoon is missing." During college, I worked as a waitress. On one of my first days, I had three tables to serve, and one customer was continually complaining, yelling, and scowling at me. At the time, I still had low self-esteem, and his reaction made me feel completely incompetent to wait tables. I felt foolish.

Fortunately, my other customers made me realize that it wasn't about me at all. First, one of my other tables paid their bill, tipping handsomely and remarking, "You truly deserve this," with a side glance at the scowling customer. As the obnoxious customer finally left, the lady at my last table said, "Poor you. Do you have many customers like that?"

Both comments made me realize that not all feedback is useful, and it is important to consider the source and motivation of the feedback before reacting to it.

Some of the feedback you get will come in the form of baseless negative remarks, as in my story above. This is useless feedback and caused by the giver simply wanting to pull down the receiver because they feel low themselves.

Checklist for Evaluating Feedback

Whenever you receive negative feedback, ask yourself the following questions:

- Is this genuine feedback? If the remarks are merely designed to hurt you, it is bullying, not feedback. In my example, my customer might have been criticized by his boss during the day and now needed to feel in charge by criticizing someone else.

- Is it based on something you could have done differently? Ask yourself the following question: If there is one valuable learning I could take from this remark, what would it be? If you can find no answer to the question, let it go. If necessary, use the methods described in this part of the book to release the hurt.

- Is this repeated feedback? The feedback you get from one person is often just their distorted perspective. If you hear the same feedback multiple times, consider if this is useful feedback you can learn from.

Feedback Jiu-Jitsu

The Japanese martial art of jiu-jitsu manipulates the opponent's force against himself instead of countering it with your own power. Feedback jiu-jitsu means accepting useless feedback without becoming defensive or inwardly angry.

A great way to handle any feedback, no matter the context, is to smile and thank the giver: "Thank you for caring enough to give me feedback. I will take it into account." Even a bully will have a hard time continuing to throw negative remarks at you, if you have the internal strength to smile and say thank you, no matter how you feel inside. Try it out. Prepare yourself ahead of time by practicing this statement. In the situation, say it and note the difference. Also, feel how it makes a difference in how you receive the feedback.

Learning from Useful Feedback

If you have determined the negative feedback has the potential to be useful, you need to be careful about how to react to it. There are two main ways we respond when we receive negative feedback:

- We allow it to block us from moving forward
  or
- We use it to evaluate our action and change course if needed.

Realize the exact same feedback can cause us to act in two completely different ways. Only when we allow negative feedback to be a moment of learning, can it become useful.

For example, your boss might give you the feedback that your work isn't accurate enough. Instead of just turning your back without knowing how to improve, thank your boss for the feedback. Ask if she would be willing to help you improve the accuracy of your work. By being willing to engage and create solutions, you are making use of the feedback to improve yourself.

Accepting Feedback

When you feel you could have done something differently, don't beat yourself up. There will always be times when this happens. Remember this essential and valid key to your life:

> *You will always do the best you can in any given situation,*
> *with the knowledge and skills you have at that time.*

Sometimes, your best is just not good enough for the situation, and this is part of life. Nobody is perfect and making mistakes is part of our learning and progress. This is what life is all about.

As you progress, you learn and gain new insights. With this new knowledge, you might choose to handle the situation differently another time. But that is because you now know something you didn't know before. The bottom line is not to beat yourself up, but to learn any lesson there is to be learned.

The best way to learn from any situation is to ask yourself, or someone you trust, if there is any learning you can take away from the feedback to improve yourself, your craft, your business, or your life. If the answer is yes, decide to learn from the feedback.

> **Lotte's Tip**
>
> When you are ready to take feedback to the next level, here is a great way to do it.
>
> Reach out to people, starting with those you feel most safe with, and ask the following question: "Where and how do you see me limiting myself?" Then brainstorm ideas to work through this and decide to take one small step towards improving yourself in this area.

Summary

Being bullied is like getting useless negative feedback. As bullying victims, we tend to discard positive feedback and accept useless negative feedback. Can you recognize this response pattern from yourself?

Life gives you a lot of feedback, some positive and some negative. Accept and appreciate the positive feedback. Smile and say thank you.

Carefully evaluate negative feedback. Remember bullies don't give useful feedback. They just want to hurt you to feel better themselves. Let go of this type of feedback. If necessary, use your favorite techniques to release any negative feelings.

If you decide you have received useful feedback, own it. Reflect on it and extract the learning.

Lotte's Strategies to Increase Your Quality of Life

- ✔ Receive compliments with an open heart, accepting them as the gifts they truly are.

- ✔ Examine negative feedback, discarding it or learning from it as appropriate. Always remember that life is a constant learning experience.

- ✔ Turn your own mistakes around, knowing you have always done the best you can with the knowledge and skills you had at that time.

Chapter 16

Forgive to Move Forward

"When you forgive, you in no way change the past – but you sure do change the future."

BERNARD MELTZER

For a long time, I struggled with the term *forgiving*. I heard over and over that you must forgive in order to move forward. But how could I possibly forgive my teacher who had caused me so much harm? She was the reason my classmates didn't want to have anything to do with me. She caused me to not believe in myself, to hate myself. There was no way I could forgive her – no way I could possibly let go of what had happened.

I finally realized what forgiving really meant. It was not about forgiving my teacher – it was about forgiving myself for holding on to my past. For being afraid to let go, for being afraid to move on, for being fearful of what might happen when I put down my shield and showed the true me. This was something entirely different and a whole new way of looking at forgiving.

Too often, we think of forgiving as an acceptance of what happened. Forgiving is quite the opposite. Forgiving is not about whether what happened to you is right or wrong. Forgiving does not mean you say that what was done to you was okay. Forgiving means acknowledging that the person didn't know any better at the time than to do what he or she did. Often, the other person is not even aware of the damage they did. Despite that, we hold on and do not allow ourselves to move forward.

To forgive is a choice. You can choose to forgive and move on, or you can choose to stay in your current situation. This might sound harsh, but the reality is that as long as we keep blaming other people, we are not taking full responsibility for our own lives. We are not giving ourselves the opportunity to release our inner blocks and move forward.

Are you ready to forgive and move forward?

For most of us, this is a long process and not something done in a day. But if you are ready to start the process, you are well on your way. For every bit of forgiving you can do, you will feel more open, have more energy, and feel freer. You can go through this process at whatever speed you want. If you do it regularly, you will move forward on your way.

There are two parts to forgiveness. The first is to forgive whoever bullied you, no matter what they did. The second is to forgive yourself for holding on to your past.

Forgiving Others

When you choose to forgive, you have different options. In this section, I will walk you through a process that has helped me in several different situations. This process is a great tool, and I encourage you to complete it several times over the next few weeks.

In this exercise, I encourage you to answer at least the first question in writing. Keeping this answer in front of you will inspire you to do the work.

For the remaining questions, you can choose to answer in writing or by saying the answer out loud or in your mind.

Exercise 28: Forgive and Let Go

1. Start by realizing who you would be without this blame towards another person?

   Write down as much as you can about what it would mean for you to let go. Who would you be? What will you be able to achieve?

2. Now ask yourself: "Am I ready to forgive this person?"

   a. If yes, move on to step 3.

   b. If no, ask yourself: "What would it take for me to be able to forgive?" Are you willing to take this step?

   c. Another option is to consider whether you would be ready to pretend that you are going to forgive? This trick takes advantage of the way our brain works. The conscious mind is just pretending, but the subconscious can't really tell the difference between pretending to forgive and actually forgiving. So, even if you initially choose to pretend you forgive, you are preparing your mind to forgive and will eventually be able to do so.

3. When you are ready to forgive, you can choose one of the following:

   a. Connect with the person, in person or by phone, and tell them directly how the bullying impacted you and that despite that, you choose to forgive them. When this is possible, it will often have a dramatic positive impact on you. Many people feel that this is too far outside their comfort zone, or they simply can't reach the person. In these cases, choose step b or c instead.

b. Write a letter to the person. State how the bullying has impacted your life and how, despite this, you choose to forgive them, let go of the past and move on with your life. Picture the person in your mind before you start to write. Putting the words down on paper makes it more real. Afterward, you can mail your letter to the person, or to tear it up, burn it, or ceremoniously bury it. Do whatever feels right for you to finish the process.

b. Visualize telling the person. Pull the person into your mind and visualize how you tell the person about their impact and how you choose to forgive. This process works very well, and many people find this to be the best way to start the process of forgiving. It is especially useful if you initially choose just to pretend that you are forgiving. The other two methods are more powerful, but you can always use them later – the important thing is that you start now.

4. Once you have completed the forgiving process, dry your tears. Most people will find tears flowing at some time during the process, and that is natural and good. Tears are healing and help you to release more deeply. Don't hold back your tears but allow them to flow freely. When you are ready, visualize your life moving forward and that you feel lighter and more powerful.

5. Congratulate yourself on taking this step and on having started the process. Repeat this process as often as you need for as long as you need to.

Forgiving Yourself

Even though it isn't easy to forgive other people, it can be even more challenging to forgive yourself for holding on to the past.

You might ask: "Why do we need to forgive ourselves?" Over my years of self-healing and helping others to heal, I have discovered that most of us have a hard time dealing with the fact we have been holding ourselves back from having a great life. Sometimes, we have been holding on to the past for 30 years or more.

No matter how long you have been held back by your past, you might be having thoughts like "Why haven't I done this before?" or "I should have…" These thoughts are also holding you back, and it is time to let them go.

The only time we have is now, in this moment. Whatever happened in the past is in the past. There is nothing you can do to make it different – but you can let it go. Now is a good time to forgive yourself for holding on to the past and start living your life to the fullness of your potential.

How is it possible to forgive yourself? How can you start this process?

The first thing is just to allow yourself to forgive. It might sound strange, but it is not as easy as it seems. We must allow ourselves to be willing to let go.

Once you are ready to forgive yourself, go through the following list of questions that will guide you through the process. Set aside a least one hour for this work, to have time to really dig deep inside of you. If you don't have time right now, scheduled a block of time in your calendar as soon as possible.

Exercise 29: Forgive Me for the Life I Have Created So Far

Answer the following questions by writing the answers in your notebook.

Who am I when I let go and allow my true self to come through?

_____

_____

Who am I when I choose to forgive and let go of the past?

_____

_____

What have I learned throughout my life that has made me the person I am today?

_____

_____

Who would I be without this experience?

_____

_____

Answering the last question made me realize that without my experiences, I would not have been as intuitive and insightful as I am today.

I cannot know where I might otherwise have been, but I do know that all the personal development, coaching, and training I have completed has made me a strong person with a unique ability to help other people. Today I am grateful for this knowledge, and I cannot imagine doing anything else with my life.

Where are you today? Who have you become? Acknowledge all the skills and the knowledge you have gained throughout your experience. Know you are who you are today because of what you have gone through. Even though you might feel weak or fearful, or have low self-esteem, there is a strong and powerful person behind all that. There is a person with a lot of knowledge and strengths waiting to come through, waiting to help other people, waiting to help you build your life on a firm foundation. Know that you are not the person you used to be – you have grown beyond that. The work you are doing now, through the exercises in this book, is helping you to let go and start building a strong foundation for a more powerful you.

Now it is time to forgive yourself, look at your answers, and realize you have learned a lot in the process. You are now ready, and in a position to move forward. Congratulations on having come this far.

Summary

Forgiving is about setting yourself free. You can choose to keep blaming your bully, or you can choose to let go and improve your life. To forgive is about allowing yourself to move forward in your life despite what happened.

Forgiving is not about whether what happened to you is right or wrong. It is about acknowledging that the person didn't know any better at the time than to do what they did. Often, the other person is not even aware of the damage they did. Despite of that, we tend to hold on and not allow ourselves to move forward.

Remember the inner wisdom you have gained from your experience as you work on forgiving your bully and yourself.

Lotte's Strategies to Increase Your Quality of Life

- ✔ Forgive your bully by acknowledging that they were not able to do any better.

- ✔ Forgive yourself for feeling you should have acted sooner.

- ✔ Acknowledge the wisdom and insights you have gained from your past.

Chapter
17

Transforming into The New You

"Life isn't about finding yourself. Life is about creating yourself."

GEORGE BERNARD SHAW

I helped my son out of the car and was turning to grab the groceries when our neighbor approached me. "Your son is so quiet," she said, "he must have gotten that from your husband because you are so outgoing and open." She couldn't possibly know what her words meant to me. A deep, profound feeling of success bubbled up in me, and I felt like shouting, "It worked."

In 1997, three years before this event, we had made a significant change in our environment. Before this shift, I had spent a year working with various personal growth self-study courses. I was very slowly making progress, but my family, friends, and coworkers still perceived me as the same old me: a quiet person, mostly keeping to herself, not very interactive or engaged in conversations. When I participated in larger events, I would usually find some practical thing to help with. If this was not possible, I would hide as best as I could in a quiet corner.

When my husband was offered the opportunity to transfer to the Switzerland office, more than 700 miles away, I took up the challenge. I decided to act as if I was the person I wanted to be. I was going to be the person I longed to be and who represented my true self at that time. The "new me" was more outgoing and ready to approach other people, no matter how hard it felt in the beginning. She was one who took chances in getting to know other people and who worked to expand her comfort zone.

I had a unique opportunity because I would meet new people who did not have any preconceived notions that I was very quiet. They would see me as the person I showed up as. Not a loud person, but one who was open and willing to speak up and interact with other people.

It was a big step to take, especially in the beginning. I forced myself to say "Yes" to every opportunity to grow. I was active in the community by participating in as many events as possible. As my German got better, more opportunities opened up, and I started a group for mothers and children in our area.

It was not easy, but it was rewarding. I would visualize how I wanted to behave as described in Chapter Seven "Envision Your Goal as Complete." When I experienced any level of fear – which was quite often in the beginning – I would work on it using the techniques in Part Three. To release fear, the following tools are especially helpful: "Tap to Release," "Regenerating Images in Memory (RIM)," and "Breathe and Let Go." I pushed through my limiting beliefs and went for it. This proved to be one of the most significant steps I had taken so far in my own recovery.

Preparing Your New Self

Who are you? Who is the real person hiding inside of you that wants to come forward and be shown to the world? Are you ready to take the next step and implement what you have learned so far to be the new you? If you are, use the following exercise that will help you start your transformation.

Think of an actor. A good actor studies his or her role in depth. They get to know the character and visualize themselves in that role.

When it is time, they will move into their role and walk, talk and *be* the person they are playing. They align themselves with the character on a deep level. The actor embodies the character.

> "*Acting is behaving truthfully under imaginary circumstances.*"

> *Sanford Meisner*

An actor is trained to move into and out of character, and you can do the same.

Our mind doesn't know the difference between real and fake. When you go through a guided visualization, you can feel the vision.

We use this to our advantage when you act as this new powerful you. The more you visualize your new behavior, the easier it becomes to implement it. Remember to feel the feelings in your body, smell the smells and hear the sounds of your surroundings. This all makes it more real and will embody experience on a deeper level.

This next exercise takes time. It is a change of your lifestyle. You might not sense much of a difference in the beginning. I promise you the transformation does occur on a deep level. The exercise is best done when you have gone through the other exercises and are ready to integrate the new you on a deeper level. It is designed to allow you to implement the changes step by step.

Exercise 30: Transforming into The New You

Go back to the vision you created in Chapter Seven. Who are you in this vision? How are you different from the person you are today? How are you interacting with other people? How are you standing, walking, dressed? What kind of people are you surrounded by? Does this vision still feel right to you? Or does it require some changes? If you feel it needs some changes, go ahead and make these changes before you take the next step. Remember your vision will change and expand over time as you grow personally. Whenever you feel the time is right to create a new vision, go ahead and do this.

Now think about a situation where you can start implementing your personal changes. The easiest way to do this is to find a new group where nobody knows the old you. Do a little research and find a group that suits you. It can be an evening class, exercise team, or church group. Anything that will fuel you and that you can look forward to is good. Feeling good will support you in implementing the change.

Visualize yourself in this group. How will you react to and interact with other people? Let your visualization take you from you walking out of your front door until you get back home. Be, do, and act as if you're already this new and powerful you. Feel the feelings you will feel when you interact with other people and feel comfortable. Hear the sounds, smell the aroma from the kitchen or the flowers. You might hear specific, empowering words. The more sensory input you can bring into your vision, the more real it gets. Play around with it and know you can keep expanding your personal vision.

Taking Off

The first day in your new group is the most important day. This is the day the other participants will see you for the first time and form their first impression of who you are. This initial impression will be the basis of their perception of you afterward.

This might feel like a big step outside your comfort zone – that is perfectly normal and okay. As you take up this challenge, your transformation will become easier afterward. Remember you only need to change as much as you are ready to. You might feel as exhausted, as though you had just run a marathon when you get back home – especially after this first day. That is to be expected because you have just spent a lot of internal energy acting and being this new you. The level of energy you need will decrease as you get into the habit of being the new you. This exercise is very powerful, and the outcome is very much worth the effort.

The great thing is that the second time you attend the same group, you will already get help from the other participants. They will now perceive you as your new you, and your mission is just to maintain and maybe add a little to their perception of you. For each meeting, you will experience that it becomes a little easier because your body starts expecting it to be this way. You will embody this new way of being in a specific environment.

When you feel comfortable in your first group, find another group or activity to expand the time you are spending as the new powerful you. Play around it. As you spend more and more time as your new you, it becomes natural and integrated into your being. I still do this exercise every time I start in a new ongoing activity, and I keep growing from it.

> **Lotte's Tip**
>
> If you are moving or changing your job, that is an excellent opportunity to transform into the new you.

Dress for Success

A simple yet powerful way to support you in your transformation is by dressing specifically for the event. For many years, I dressed in unflattering, too-large clothes so I could hide. When I started to dress more in tune with my body, I felt more empowered. Choose to use clothes as actors do. Putting on a specific "costume" tells your body how you want to feel. This works exceptionally well when you choose to feel these feelings as you change your clothes.

Find out what clothes, shoes, and accessories will make you feel most comfortable and powerful. Wear this style every time you are acting out your new role. You might even want to go out and buy a few new items. It will be a worthwhile investment. Dress for the event you are going to take part in and dress in a way that supports you to embody your new you. Our appearance not only sends signals to others that we are worth connecting with, it also sends subtle, yet powerful messages to our own subconscious mind. When you dress for the occasion, you support your internal growth.

Creating Supportive Surroundings

My clients often experience that their workplace is a challenge. Your colleagues only know the old you. They are so used to this outdated version of you that it will take them a while to recognize the change you have made.

Take it easy with the changes at work. Implement your changes elsewhere and incorporate them. As you change and grow, your colleagues will slowly transform their way of looking at you. The same will be true for family and friends you haven't told about your inner journey.

I invite you to invite your closest family into your journey – the people you are sharing your household with. You are spending a lot of time with them, and you want them to support your change, not see the old you. Are there other people you want to let in on this? Maybe your best friends? It can be helpful to have someone you can talk to about the ups and downs in this transformation.

Family gatherings can be a challenge. In the beginning, I would sometimes even cry when I got back home from a family event because I felt I hadn't changed at all. In these situations, I found it very useful to have the support of my husband. He could help me see all the places where I had indeed changed, and with his help, I was able to see myself in a new light.

Your family will initially see and treat you as your old self, and this can cause you to fall out of the new character and start acting in the old way. As you feel more secure in your new role, the change becomes more noticeable, and it will be easier to stay true to your new self. Eventually, even old friends and family members will start seeing and responding to your new self.

Summary

Transform yourself into the new you by starting to act as if you already are this person. Participate in groups where you can meet new people and be, act, and dress as the person you are aiming to be.

Use this exercise to gradually feel more secure and at ease being the new powerful you. Every new situation is an opportunity to grow. The more you practice, the easier it becomes.

Lotte's Strategies to Increase Your Quality of Life

✔ Find a group that inspires you. This will make it easier to take the next step towards the life you desire.

✔ Dress for success. When you are ready, go through your wardrobe and discard all clothes you don't feel powerful in. When you go shopping, buy clothes that support the new you.

✔ Enlist support from other people. This can be your family, friends, a coach, or online support groups.

Chapter
18

Who Do You Surround Yourself With?

"The biggest adventure you can take is to live the life of your dreams."

OPRAH WINFREY

Before you read this chapter, I want you to close your eyes and think about the five people you spend the most time together with. This might not be your family but can be colleagues or people in your community.

As you think about these people, notice how you interact with each other. What do you talk about? How do you treat each other? How do you support each other? Write down a few notes about your experience just to remember before you read on. Well done.

I had a client once, who wanted to stop drinking. She had realized she had a problem and wanted to quit. It all went very well for a time, she kept her goal and took her medicine. Then one day she told me: "I don't want to keep this goal. I'm going to stop taking my medicine."

I felt sure she still wanted to quit drinking – otherwise, she would have started to drink again before our session. Inquiring deeper, I discovered that her best friend kept telling her that to stop drinking was a stupid goal. And the friend was drinking way too much. Not wanting to face his own demons, he was encouraging his friend to keep drinking.

Beware of the People Holding You Back

People with low self-esteem might attempt to use you to raise their self-esteem. This usually happens unconsciously, and most of these people have their own traumatic experiences to deal with. In fact, people who bully often have low self-esteem and use bullying to feel their own power.

People who suffer from the effect of being bullied
are at risk of being used to raise other people's self-esteem.

Today, as you have taken responsibility for your own life, some of your friends might feel threatened by your new behavior and higher self-esteem. Be aware that your friends and family members might try to pull you away from your new path. Limit the time you spend with these people. Remember that they are doing it unconsciously and can't help it.

When you have a hard time establishing friendships, you are happy when someone, anyone, wants to be your best friend. But if your best friend is trying to hold you back from your self-development journey, read the signals and take a closer look at what is happening. Trust your intuition and trust that you are on the right path. Don't allow anyone to hold you back. Keep going and seek support in other places.

The Five Most Important People in Your Life

Research shows that the five people we are around the most, influence us the most. Who are the five people that influence you the most? Look at the five names that you wrote down at the beginning of this chapter. Look at each name and ask yourself: is this person supportive of me or holding me back? Be honest in your answer.

When the people you spend the most time with are mainly complaining about their current circumstances, it is easy for you to also just complain and be dragged into this negative spiral.

If for example you smoke, and during all the breaks at work, you hang around your colleges who smoke. Now imagine you want to quit smoking and are still spending time with your smoking coworkers. How easy do you think it will be for you to keep your goal of stopping smoking?

Now imagine that you just quit smoking and during breaks, you spend time with people who aren't smoking and spend the time in non-smoking areas. Obviously, this will make it much easier to stick to your goal.

Make a habit of being aware of the people that surround you and how you're interacting with each other. Make a note of those you find are supportive and uplifting to be with. Start spending more time with supportive people and less time with the people you find are holding you back.

Exercise 31: Who Supports You?

- Make a list of all the people you spend significant time with. Include family, friends, and coworkers.

- Now mark each person with a plus or minus sign. + for uplifting – for holding you back.

- Look at each name and think about how you can either increase or limit the time you spend with this person. The goal is to spend as much time as possible with supportive and uplifting people.

- Write down at least one change you can do today to spend more time with supportive people

_____

_____

How to Find Supportive People

Look at the activities you are currently participating in – work, sports, associations, voluntary work. Are these groups supportive or do they tend to be blaming and complain a lot? Be honest. If necessary, start looking out for new opportunities that might be a better fit for you.

It can sometimes be easier to find people who are more uplifting and supportive outside of your current environment. One way to find support is to participate in meetup groups, hobbies, or sports activities, etc. These are usually an excellent place to find like-minded people and can be very beneficial, especially if you have no other support.

Think about what you love to do. What gives you energy? Uplifts your mood? What do you really want to learn? Look for these kinds of activities in your area.

Self-development programs with longer duration can also be a good source of uplifting, development-oriented people. Look for multi-day events away from home or groups with regular meetings throughout multiple months.

We often spend quite a lot of time with our colleges at work. Do your best to devote more time to those colleges who are uplifting and inspiring. If you can't find any, you might want to spend break time going for a walk instead of hanging around negative people.

Take small steps and start spending more time with more supportive people. Little by little as you change, you will become one of the people others seek out for being supportive and uplifting.

Summary

Having support in your surroundings is essential. When we are surrounded by people who spend their lives blaming and complaining, it is easy to join them. Make a list of the five people you spend the most time with and evaluate if these are supportive of you or holding you back. Be on the lookout for uplifting and supporting people and start spending more time with them. And limit the time you spend with people who are holding you back.

Lotte's Strategies to Increase Your Quality of Life

- ✔ Take a look at the people you are surrounded by on a regular basis.

- ✔ Get into the habit of spending your time with more uplifting and supportive people.

- ✔ What is one change you can do this month to spend more time with people who support you? Make a commitment to make one small change. When you do this each month, in one year from now you will notice your surroundings have changed.

Chapter
19

Take the Next Step

"Today I choose life. Every morning when I wake up, I can choose joy, happiness, negativity, pain... To feel the freedom that comes from being able to continue to make mistakes and choices - today I choose to feel life, not to deny my humanity but embrace it."

KEVYN AUCOIN

I commend you for your willingness and commitment to healing and moving forward. Taking action is the most important thing you can do when you want to change.

I hope you have found time to do the exercises outlined as you read the book. If not, I highly recommend you revisit the ones you haven't done yet and try them. The most significant shift will happen when you do the exercises.

You have started a journey, and now you want to continue on your road to success. The *Life After Bullying* book is designed to be a combined roadmap and toolbox. Keep it handy, and use the tools described as you move forward. Re-read the book occasionally when you are ready to take the next step. Each time you read the book, you will discover new things you didn't notice the first time through. And in redoing the exercises, you will achieve a new level of understanding yourself and will find out what the next step will be for you.

Remember to visit the book website www.lifeafterbullying.com. There, you find not only the workbook with all the exercises but also audio and video guides for some of the exercises and techniques and a list of other resources to use in your journey.

If you feel you want more, you also find the online *Life After Bullying* program on the book website. This is based on the content of the book, and with more time and all the possibilities of an online course, I can take the information presented in the book a step further.

I honor you for the work you do, and I am looking forward to hearing about your success. Feel free to send me an email to lotte@ lifeafterbullying.com with your story and results.

I wish you joy and happiness in the years to come.

Lotte

Index

A

accepting
  myself 26
  responsibility 22
  the past 37
  your situation 39
achieving goals 11
acknowledge 19, 37, 38, 39, 43, 45, 51, 171, 181
act as if 211, 214
action 17
  outcome from 186
  plan 112, 113
  steps 106, 115
  taking 17, 225
acupressure 146
addiction 26
addictions 82
affirmation 120
anchoring
  vision 33, 120
anorexia 26
anxiety xxi, 3, 7, 22, 24, 46, 47, 62, 131, 145, 154, 161
  reducing with tapping 146
appearance 216
appreciation 6

B

behaviors, holding on to new 16
belief 30, 31
  embedded 40

lack of 4
limiting 3, 26, 29, 31, 40, 41, 43, 45, 95, 145, 178
muscle 31, 54
strengthening physically 191
blaming 25, 26
  my first teacher 22
  stopping 24
  yourself 26, 27, 66
blocked, by fear 17
block, mental 31
blueprint for success 78
body
  different feeling 32
  reactions 160
brain 10, 47, 98, 117, 161
break, taking 17
breakthrough 23
breathing 65, 168, 169, 170
  shallow 167
buddy, supportive 30
bulimia 26
bullying xix, xxi, xxii, 23, 24, 25, 37
  impact 131

C

calm, feeling 55, 175
calming breathing 168
Canfield, Jack 25, 183
capable
  feeling 4, 22, 51
  not feeling 24

celebrate 136
celebrating 16
challenge
    family gatherings 217
    moving to a different
        country 211
    physical 190
change xxvi, 3, 5, 6, 7, 17, 19, 24, 25
    being recognized 216
    necessary 22
    taking responsibility 22
changing job, as opportunity to
    transform 216
choice 5, 22, 24, 48
    making your own 24
Chunyi Lin 35
climbing 16, 18, 189, 191
coach 25, 191
    working with 16
colleagues
    knowing the old you 216
    transforming their view 217
comfort 65
    eating 25, 82
    zone xxi, 56, 62, 65, 93, 102,
        110, 177, 178, 181, 190
    zone, expanding
        physically 191
    zone, goal outside 101
commitment 7, 8, 20, 45, 144, 225
    cost of 141
compassion 22
complaining 24

D

daily habit, mirror exercise 69
dancing 56, 58
deadline

far in the future 112
    for goal 101
Deborah Sandella xx, 159
decision 3, 4, 5, 6, 25, 27, 31, 142
    conscious belief 157
    to change 22
depression 161
desire 18, 79, 81, 92
difference, making a 53
discomfort, noticing 9
discovering things to be grateful
    for 9
don't do list 141
dream xix, 9, 23, 92, 93, 96
dressing, as the new you 216

E

EFT 145
Emotional Freedom
    Technique 145
emotions
    from saying no 141
    negative 146
    stuck 132, 160
    supressing 6, 38
    unlocking 6
    working on 145
empowering 33
energy 83, 84, 87, 139
    freeing 38
    higher 173
    increasing 56
    stuck 146
energy points 146
event 25, 26
excuse 24, 142, 154
exercise 65

acknowledge your current
    situation 44
action plan 113
breathing to relax 169
buy a journal 10
changing your reactions 28
commitment to the process 8
create a list of your deepest
    wishes 96
create your own
    affirmation 121
discovering your
    uniqueness 52
dream 94
enhance your voice 164
envisioning your goal
    achieved 119
finding yourself 19, 20
find meaning in your life 85
forgive and let go 205
forgive me for the life I have
    created so far 208
how do I spend my day? 137
minimum/target/outrageous
    goals 115
mirror exercise 68, 69
my daily life 140
notice how you feel 49
placing your voice 64
preparing for success 33
relax and let go 174
release your thoughts 171
setting a clear and measurable
    goal 103
start journaling 12
take a step outside your
    comfort zone 185
transforming into the new
    you 214

uncover your limiting
    beliefs 41
    who supports you 221
experience 24, 27, 47, 74
    lived 29
    sharing 133
    visualized 29

F

failure, setting up for 30
family xxii, 8, 16, 40, 138, 139
    improved relationships 67
    inviting into your journey 217
    seeing the old you 211, 217
fear 3, 5, 6, 17, 18, 22, 167, 181
    moving through 182
feeling 7, 10, 16, 18, 65, 154
    anxious 34
    insecure 37
    peace 55
    releasing 39
    tapping beyond 153
flashbacks 160
focus 46, 47, 48, 84
    improved 173
forgiving 25, 26
    yourself 207, 209
foundation xxv, xxvi, 18
    for success 78
friends 16
    seeing the old you 211
    struggling to find 22
    supporting 138
    threatened by new
        behavior 220
fulfilled, feeling 86
fulfilling life 139
future xxvi, 94, 95

G

goal xxv, xxvi, 9, 77, 78, 99
    achieving 109
    action steps 106, 111
    affirmation 120
    aligned with values 92
    evaluating 79
    for personal growth 102
    setting 92
    SMART 100
    stretch 101
    weight loss 26
Goodbye Hurt & Pain (book) 160
GPS xxvi, 79, 99, 117
grief 40
group, joining new 215
growth 24, 38
    by pushing 181
    personal xxi, 9, 41, 102, 110, 190, 211
guide 191
    lack of 6
guilt 66

H

habit
    changing 26
    daily mirror exercise 69
    getting rid of 83
healing xix, xxii, xxv, xxvi, 5, 6, 7, 8, 24, 39, 45, 225
    by taking back time 139
Himalaya 15, 18
hobbies, source of supportive people 222
hopeful, feeling 55

I

ideal life 77, 94
impact 5
improvement 8, 9
    keeping track of 9
index card, for goal 122
insecure 32, 46
    feeling 37
integrity, loss of 135
intention, breathing exercise 170
internal shift 29
intuition 5, 133
    following 85, 96
    trusting 220

J

Jack Canfield 25, 183
journal
    on computer 10
    paper 10
journaling 9, 12, 17, 52, 55, 57, 133, 157, 180
    habit 12
    overcoming limiting belief 31
journey xix, xxii, xxv, xxvi, xxvii, 5, 6, 7, 15, 16, 17, 18, 19, 74, 225
    friends holding you back 220
    keeping track of 9
joy xxv, 22, 58, 86
just for now 171

K

keeping track 133

L

Law of Attraction 46

letting go xix
life 23
    evaluating 79
    fulfilling xxviii, 139
    full of joy 22
    impact on 5
    my own 3
    new xxv, 15
    on autopilot 137
    owning 19
    purpose xxi
    quality xxv
    turning around 40
    value 78
Lin, Chunyi 35
love yourself 67, 68, 71, 139, 143

M

meaning 86
    adding to your life 88
meditation xxi, 173, 175
meetup groups, source of
    supportive people 222
memory, emotional 161
mental
    drawer 172
    pain 22
Michelangelo 8
milestones 11
    planned 11
    spontaneous 11
mind 46
    training 25
mirror exercise 68, 69, 180
mission, my own 97
mood
    changing 56
motivation 80

mountain 15, 17, 91
movement 55
moving house, as opportunity to
    transform 216

N

nervous 46
New Year, dream exercise 93
no, saying 141
notebook, always carrying 147
notice 9, 27, 31, 47, 65

O

obstacles 18
    addressing 111
    creating 30
outcome 24, 25, 26, 186
    negative, imagined 29
ownership 19, 51
    of your life 27

P

pain 7
    mental 22
partner 16
passion xxi
    living 40
peace 47, 54, 55
    inner 55, 74
people 65, 154
    supporting 23
    uplifting 221
    you spend most time with 220
playing 55, 56, 57, 58
pleaser syndrome 135, 141, 142
possibility
    from action 186
    of change 32

of something better 104

power 6, 24, 29, 74
    giving to yourself 38

preparing xxvi

process xxii, xxv, 5, 6, 7, 8, 31, 45
    forgiving 207, 209
    slow 8

progress xxvi, xxviii, 8, 10, 11,
    55, 211
    hard to measure 92
    noting 180
    physical embodiment 191

Q

Qigong 35

quality of life xxii, 143

R

reaction 24, 25, 26, 27

recipe for success 184

recovery 15, 17

Regenerating Images in Memory
    xix, 159

relaxed, feeling 55

relaxing 55, 58, 168

releasing 39
    blocks 164

responsibility 22, 24, 25, 28
    accepting 22

resting 72

rewarding yourself 181

RIM xix, xx, 159, 161, 162, 164
    exercise 164
    facilitator 161

roadblocks xxvi

S

safety

creating 162

Sandella, Deborah xx, 159

self-care 67

self-centered 67

self-confidence, improving
    physically 191

self-doubt, reducing with
    tapping 146

self-esteem xxi, 31
    goal 102
    low 4, 26, 38, 131
    raising 24, 26

self-hatred 66

self-help tool 145, 146

self-image 20

self-study course 211

self-worth xix, 31
    low 4, 19, 38

serving others 142

sexual abuse 26

sharing 16
    your story 39

shield
    putting down 55

situation
    current 22, 37, 40

sleep 4, 9
    disorder 131
    improved 173

social anxiety xix, xxi, 46, 131

source of supportive people 222

speaking xxi, 62

sports activities, source of
    supportive people 222

steps, small 65

stress 24, 135, 161, 167
    bouncing back 168
    decreasing 74

subconsciously 46

success 30, 78, 225, 226
    recipe 184
    setting up for 30
    stories 133
suicide 40
support xxv, xxvi, 6, 16, 30, 31
    from other people 221, 222
    physical 190
supporting other people 40, 54, 97
Switzerland 211
symptoms 131

T

taking action 225
talents 51, 54
    lack of belief in 4
tapping 124, 145, 146, 147, 148, 154
    beyond the immediate
        feeling 153
    body reaction 154
    choice method 155
    example 152
    final measuring 152
    initial measuring 148
    journaling 157
    MP3 audio file 155
    points 151
    set-up statement 149
    statements 152
    tapping rounds 150
    video 152
task, aligned with values 141
teacher 3, 4, 22, 24, 37
time 65, 154
    creating 139, 142, 144
    difficult 16
    freeing up 137, 141
    how do you spend 137

quality 139
    spent wisely 138
    taking time to rest 72
tools xix, xxv, xxvi, 5, 6, 7,
        132, 225
    self-help 145
transformation 7, 10, 16, 22, 217
    supporting by dressing 216
trauma xix, xxi, 24, 131, 160
    accessing roots 159
traumatic memories, handling 162
treasures 84
trust 5, 162
    in yourself 30
    lack of 4, 22
    necessary for speaking 63

U

uncomfortable 32
uniqueness 48, 51
unworthy, feeling 18, 24

V

values 84
    core 88
virtual resource 162
vision xxi, 33, 91, 93
    my own 116
    yours 117
vision board 122
visualizing 33, 94, 214
    different response 27, 29
voice xix, 61, 62, 65
    freeing 72
    hushed 131
    joining a choir 63
    losing 4, 37
    missing link 62

placing 64
practicing 65
volunteering 138

W

walls, pushing 177, 181
website xxvii
weight
    gaining 25
    losing 26
    loss, goal 80
    struggling with 25
win 9, 16, 136
wisdom 74
wish 100
wish list 96
workplace, as a transformation
        challenge 216
worst case scenario, never
        happening 186
worthy of living 40

About the Author

As a bullied child, Lotte W. Vesterli could barely speak. Through hard work with many mentors, she has found her voice again and now enjoys helping others find theirs.

Lotte is a trained occupational therapist specialized in cognitive dysfunctions. She worked with younger people with acquired brain injuries for many years and built up a whole team for this work.

Later Lotte became a master and trainer in RIM (Regenerating Images in Memory), a master NLP and transformational coach and Certified Canfield Trainer in the Success Principles. She is a co-author of the book *Success University for Woman* and is a member of the Trauma Support Group of the Danish Jewish Society.

Devoted to supporting people all over the world to heal from their traumatic past, Lotte started her own practice in 2012. Today Lotte is an international speaker, has online programs, and works with private clients worldwide. Lotte conducts training and workshops on personal growth and works with businesses to improve their psychological work environment.

Lotte is married with two grown children. She lives near Copenhagen and enjoys sea kayaking along the coastline of Denmark.

Learn more about Lotte, her programs and her work with individual clients at www.lottevesterli.com.

Lightning Source UK Ltd.
Milton Keynes UK
UKHW041252060119
334994UK00002B/5/P